Children's Museums

To my grandchildren, who love to see,
do, touch, explore and imagine.
Thank you for sharing many of those times with me.
Grandpa would have been proud of you all.

CHILDREN'S MUSEUMS

An American Guidebook

by JOANN NORRIS

McFarland & Company, Inc., Publishers
Jefferson, North Carolina, and London

ALSO BY JOANN NORRIS AND JOHN R. NORRIS

The Historic Railroad: A Guide to
Museums, Depots and Excursions in the United States
(McFarland, 1996)

Amusement Parks: An American Guidebook, 2d ed.
(McFarland, 1994)

Cover: The Maritime Aquarium at Norwalk, Connecticut
(photo: Jim Herity)

British Library Cataloguing-in-Publication data are available

Library of Congress Cataloguing-in-Publication Data

Norris, Joann, 1947–
    Children's museums : an American guidebook / by Joann Norris.
      p. cm.
    Includes index.
    ISBN 0-7864-0443-4 (sewn softcover : 50# alk. paper) ∞
    1. Children's museums — United States — Guidebooks.   I. Title.
AM11.N67   1998
069'.083 — dc21   97-42194
                                                     CIP

Manufactured in the United States of America

McFarland & Company, Inc., Publishers
 Box 611, Jefferson, North Carolina 28640

CONTENTS

ACKNOWLEDGMENTS

A special thanks to all of the curators who provided information for this book, not just about their own museums but about other museums of which they had knowledge (and thought I might not). Thanks for your professionalism and helpfulness, not only to me, but to your peers.

PREFACE

The Children's Museum in Indianapolis is the largest children's museum in the United States, with 24,000 sq. ft. of floor space and an average yearly attendance of over 1,000,000 people. Most children's museums' statistics, however, come nowhere close to these figures. This does not mean that a visit to one of the smaller museums would not be beneficial, both for fun and educational purposes. My husband and I took our children to the Indianapolis museum in the early 1980s. Two years ago, we took our grandchildren to a small museum in Sebring, Florida. It's hard to say which day (or which group of children) was the most enjoyable (probably the grandchildren!). The Indianapolis museum is a member of several associations, but smaller museums tend not to spend their tightly budgeted monies on association memberships. Because they are not affiliated with any associations (see Appendix) it may be difficult for the nation's public to find out about them. I knew that it would take a lot of time and research to seek out these smaller museums. The 242 museums listed in this book are current children's museums, both large and small, for which I was able to obtain information; my hope is that parents will use the information given here to plan quality family time with their children, whether it be a single morning excursion or part of a larger vacation experience. Included in each listing is information about other sites of interest fairly near the museum.

My first research stop was the *Official Museum Directory* which listed more than 275 children's museums. I wrote to all of these museums (some of which had closed) to obtain information, and many of them sent me names of other museums with which they were affiliated in some way, or that they simply knew about "through the grapevine." I also checked with other museum list books, newspapers and magazines which carried stories on specific museums, or children's museums in general. I am fully aware that there may be other smaller museums that are not included (possibly even some larger ones). The author would be appreciative of receiving any information about any museum not included in this listing.

I would also suggest looking in the annual *Official Museum Directory* for museums listed under "Village Museums," "Folk Art Museums," "Toy and Doll Museums," "Wax Museums," "Whaling Museums" and a vast number of others that might interest your children and you.

INTRODUCTION

All museums listed in this book claim to have participatory, interactive, hands-on exhibits and or displays of specific interest to children, or to have formally organized education programs especially for children.

In the mission statement provided by most of the 242 museums listed in this book, the intent of the museum staff and other personnel is to provide a safe and free place where children can see, touch, do, explore, create, imagine, and interact with their environment, thereby learning more than might be possible in a more structured environment. According to Howard Gardner, professor of education and co-director of Project Zero at Harvard University, this kind of learning can greatly influence their work as they get older. He says:

> I think the museum for young people is one of the most hopeful institutions in the world today. The youth museum gives more people a chance to develop their intelligences and to find out what they can do both for themselves and for their community — how they can develop abilities which can not only be productive for them, but which can be productive for others…. [They] can really help kids go beyond the unschooled mind, to engender genuine understanding, while at the same time preserving the best of the five-year-old mind. If kids have a chance to go to children's museums or discovery museums to learn about their own minds, the kinds of things they can do and what it means to discover stuff, they really have the best chance to do creative work when they're older.

The oldest children's museums in the United States opened in Boston and Brooklyn around the turn of the century. Growth was slow, but today, children's museums are a growing venture in the United States, and, indeed, the world. Although there were only a dozen or so well-known museums in the 1970s, a large number of museums opened in the 1980s. The numbers have not changed as dramatically since then because many small museums close and open each year, but larger museums and even smaller museums are continually adding to and or changing exhibits, increasing both the size and the scope of the visitors' experience possibilities. More and more communities are becoming aware of the need for educational facilities which will increase the influence of what their children are learning in their formal schooling experience, and, hopefully, the number of quality museums will continue to increase.

It is difficult to really get an accurate record of how many children's museums are currently in existence. From the beginning of the research part of this book until publication, some museums have closed and others have opened — largely because of a lack of funding. Most children's museums, hoping to attract families and school groups, require only small entrance fees (some have no fees at all). It seems logical, then, that funding has to come from outside sources and is essential in keeping the museum running. (Becoming a member of the ASTC or the AYM can help provide information about such funding — see Appendix.)

It is strongly suggested that you call or FAX the museum shortly before your visit for current information, especially about hours and admissions costs. Many of the larger museums also have websites or E-mail addresses which are included in their listing and from which you can obtain current information. Many museums cater especially to school groups and will close to the public when a school group is in attendance, so you would not be able to visit at that time. Many museums also require advanced reservations because they are run by volunteers who work only when there is a reservation scheduled.

Admissions fees listed are for individuals and were valid in 1997. Nearly all museums do offer special group rates, and teachers can use the information in these listings to contact the museums for current group rates.

MUSEUM
INFORMATION

(BY STATE)

Alabama

Children's Hands-on Museum
Tuscaloosa, Alabama

Participatory education is the goal of the Children's Hands-on Museum. Two to twelve year olds and their caregivers are the targeted audience. High quality, entertaining and interactive exhibits and programs emphasize the community, the physical environment, science, history, and the arts.

Staff and volunteers are on the premises to answer questions on the exhibits which include "Choctaw Indian Village," "First National Bank of Tuscaloosa," "Maxwell General Store," "Print Shop," Barber's Shop," "Grandmother's Attic," "Planetarium," "Children's Hospital," "TV Studio," "Captain Tim Park," "Images," "Citizenship Center," "Beavers' Bends," and more.

Info in brief: Hands-on, participatory museum for children and their caregivers.

Location: 2213 University Boulevard in downtown Tuscaloosa.

Hours: Tuesday–Friday, 9 A.M. to 5 P.M.; Saturday, 1 P.M. to 5 P.M.

Admissions: Under 3, free; all others, $3. Children must be accompanied by adults.

Other sites of interest nearby: Paul W. Bryant Museum, the Alabama Museum of Natural History, the University of Alabama Arboretum, The Mercedes-Benz U.S. International Visitors Center (spring of 1997).

For further information write to Children's Hands-on Museum, P.O. Box 1672, Tuscaloosa, Alabama 35403, or call (205) 349-4235 or FAX (205) 349-4276.

Discovery 2000
Birmingham, Alabama

For further information contact: Discovery 2000, 1320 22nd St. South, Birmingham, Alabama 35206, phone: (205) 558-2000. Member ASTC.

The Exploreum Museum of Science
Mobile, Alabama

For further information contact: The Exploreum Museum of Science, 1906 Springhill Ave., Mobile, Alabama 36607, phone: (334) 471-5923. Member ASTC.

Alaska

The Imaginarium
Anchorage, Alaska

The Imaginarium, opened in 1987, is a "Science Discovery Center for All Ages." Exhibits include "Spectacles," "Physics of Toys," "Marine Life Touch Tank," "Bubbles," "Arctic Life and the Polar Bear Lair," "Galaxy Room & Planetarium," and "Science Park" (an open science lab with lots of hands-on experiment stations).

Info in brief: A hands-on science museum for children and their caregivers.

Location: Downtown Anchorage, across from the Westmark Hotel.

Hours: Monday–Saturday, 10 A.M. to 6 P.M.; Sunday, noon to 5 P.M. Closed all major holidays.

Admissions: Under 2, free; children (2–12), $4; adults, $5; seniors, $4. Memberships available. Member ASTC.

For further information write to The Imaginarium, 725 West Fifth Avenue, Anchorage, Alaska 99501, or call (907) 276-3179.

Arizona

Arizona Museum for Youth
Mesa, Arizona

The Arizona Museum for Youth is a public/private partnership between the City of Mesa and the Arizona Museum for Youth Friends, Inc. The goal of the museum, since its inception in 1978, has been to introduce "children to the visual excitement and cultural enrichment provided by fine arts." Holding its first exhibit experience in 1981, the museum is now one of only two museums in the United States with a fine arts focus. In its current facility — a 17,000 sq. ft. former grocery store — the museum now offers a unique program of workshops, classes and special events along with its exhibitions.

The display of the exhibits themselves is a unique concept. Three times each year, the entire museum is transformed (or re-transformed) into a water park, a ranch, a foreign country, a zoo, a Broadway theatre, or even a grocery store. All existing exhibits are interspersed with participatory activities which reinforce and enhance the visual experience always offered. Local merchants and community members often donate articles for these displays which encourage hands-on, creative play.

Info in brief: Unique hands-on fine arts museum for children, offering visual and tactile experiences.

Hours: (Fall & spring exhibits) Tuesday–Friday and Sunday, 1 P.M. to 5 P.M.; Saturday, 10 A.M. to 5 P.M.; (summer exhibits) Tuesday–Friday, 9 A.M. to 5 P.M.; Saturday, 10 A.M. to 5 P.M.; Sunday, 1 P.M. to 5 P.M.

Admissions: Under 2, free; others, $2.

Unique exhibitions: Three museum-wide participatory exhibits offered each year, each based on a theme with an emphasis on the fine arts.

Other sites of interest nearby: Tourist attractions in Phoenix and Mesa.

For further information write to the Arizona Museum for Youth, 35 N. Robson St., Mesa, Arizona 85201, or call (602) 644-2467.

Arizona Science Center
Phoenix, Arizona

The Arizona Science Center is a hands-on science museum for children. Exhibits include activities on energy, physics, the human body, bubbles, weather and more. Live science demonstrations are offered regularly, along with special programs and workshops. An ice cream shop is also on site.

Info in brief: A hands-on children's museum.

Hours: Monday–Saturday, 9 A.M. to 5 P.M.; Sunday, noon to 5 P.M.

Admissions: Contact museum for current admissions charges.

For further information write to the Arizona Science Center, 147 E. Adams St., Phoenix, Arizona 85004-2394, or call (602) 256-9388.

Hall of Fame Museum of Firefighting
Phoenix, Arizona

Children can explore all aspects of the 1916 fire engine on display at the Hall of Fame Museum of Firefighting. Over 100 other pieces of vintage firefighting apparatus and equipment are also on display with several fire engines on view from various countries around the world. Besides the 1916 fire engine, several hands-on fire safety exhibits are also available for children to experience.

Info in brief: Special interest collections museum with several hands-on exhibits for children.

Hours: Monday–Saturday, 9 A.M. to 5 P.M.; Sunday, noon to 4 P.M.

Admissions: Small admissions charge.

Unique exhibits: Exhibits dedicated to firefighting apparatus, equipment and history.

Other sites of interest nearby (in Phoenix): Arizona Science Center, Arizona Doll and Toy Museum, Arizona Hall of Fame Museum, Deer Valley Rock Art Center, Desert Botanical Garden, The Heard Museum, Heritage Square, The Medical Museum, Museo Chicano, Phoenix Art Museum, Phoenix Museum of History, Phoenix Police Museum, The Phoenix Zoo, Pioneer Arizona Living History Museum, Plotkin Judaica Museum of Greater Phoenix, Pueblo Grande Museum, Shemer Art Center and Museum, Telephone Pioneer Museum, and other Phoenix tourist attractions.

For further information write to Hall of Fame Museum of Firefighting, 6101 E. Van Buren, Phoenix, Arizona 85008-3450, or call (602) ASK-FIRE (275-3473).

Halle Heart Center
at the American Heart Association
Tempe, Arizona

This small museum gives children and adult visitors an interesting hands-on way of learning about cardiovascular disease (the number one cause of death in the United States) and its prevention. Contact the museum before visiting.

Info in brief: Special interest education center/museum for people of all ages, but with definite hands-on activities for children and their caregivers.

Hours: Monday–Friday, 10 A.M. to 5 P.M.

Admissions: Free.

Unique exhibits: All exhibits dedicated to teaching about cardiovascular disease and its prevention.

Other sites of interest nearby (in Tempe): Arizona Historical Society, Arizona State University Art Museum (and other sites on campus), Salt River Project History Center, Tactile Museum for the Blind & Visually Impaired (mobile), Tempe Art Center and Sculpture Garden, Tempe Historical Museum, Niels Petersen House Museum, and the Island of Big Surf water park.

For further information write to Halle Heart Center at the American Heart Association, 2929 S. 48th St., Tempe, Arizona 85282-3145, or call (602) 414-5353.

Pioneer Arizona Living History Museum
Phoenix, Arizona

Pioneer Arizona was actually in the planning for about 13 years before officially opening its doors in 1969. Current plans call for further additions and improvements to the facilities. The nonprofit museum's collection of original and reconstructed buildings currently displays various architecture and lifestyles from throughout Arizona, and encourages learning through the participatory living history concept.

Exhibits include the Saloon, Restaurant, Gift Shop, Opera House, Farm Machine Display, Carpenter Shop, Victorian House, Print Shop, Dress Shop, Exhibit of Weapons, Tinware & Locks, Blacksmith, Farm House, Miners Cabin, Arista (ore grinder), Bandstand, Church, Teacherage, School House, Cemetery, Stage Stop (Ruins), Ranch Complex & Spring House & Root Cellar, Barn & Corral, Flying V Cabin, Ashurst Cabin, Presidio & Spanish Colonial Horses, Northern Complex, Last Chance Saloon, Southern House, Sheriff's Office, Bank, Wagonmaker Shop (Ruins), and Rock Wall.

Info in brief: An educational, living history museum of interest to the entire family.

Location: 30 min. north of downtown Phoenix on Interstate 17.

For further information write to Pioneer Arizona, 3901 W. Pioneer Rd., Phoenix, Arizona 85027, or call (602) 993-0212.

Silva House
Phoenix, Arizona

One of the group of houses open in Heritage Square (original townsite of Phoenix), the Silva House is maintained by the Salt River Project, and all exhibits in the house focus on the history of water and electric power use in the Valley along with local turn-of-the-century lifestyles. Activities for children change according to the educational focus of the museum for that time. Be sure to contact the museum before visiting.

Since opening in 1980, the main focus of the Silva House has been community service to school and other groups, but exhibits and activities are also open to the public. The targeted groups are school age children and their caregivers.

Info in brief: One part of a living history museum (Heritage Square) which has some activities for children and their caregivers.

Location: In historic Heritage Square, the original townsite to Phoenix, listed on the National Register of Historic Places.

Hours: Monday–Saturday, 10 A.M. to 4 P.M.; Sunday, noon to 4 P.M.

Admissions: Free.

Unique exhibits: All exhibits are approved by the Salt River Project and emphasize water and electric power use in the Valley.

Other sites of interest nearby (in Phoenix): (See the Hall of Fame Museum of Firefighting entry.)

For further information write to the Silva House, 628 E. Adams, Phoenix, Arizona 85004, or call (602) 236-5451.

Telephone Pioneer Museum
Phoenix, Arizona

The history of telecommunications from the 1870s to today in Arizona is exhibited in interactive displays at the Telephone Pioneer Museum in Phoenix. Both permanent and changing exhibits are on display throughout the year. Changing exhibits include photographs, hand tools, switchboards, coin phones, directories, telegraphs, teletypes, Bell system memorabilia and archival materials.

Info in brief: A special interest museum with interactive displays for all ages.

Hours: Monday–Friday, 8 A.M. to 5 P.M.

Admissions: Free.

Unique exhibits: All exhibits help trace the history of telecommunications in Arizona.

Other sites of interest nearby (in Phoenix): (See the Hall of Fame Museum of Firefighting entry.)

For further information write to the Telephone Pioneer Museum, U.S. West Communication, 20 E. Thomas Rd., Phoenix, Arizona 85012-3103, or call (602) 630-2060.

Tempe Historical Museum
Tempe, Arizona

The Tempe Historical Museum is an historical museum depicting the history of Tempe from its founding in 1871 to the present. Several hands-on exhibits are offered, including a 40-foot model showing water development in the desert.

Info in brief: A history museum with several hands-on exhibits for children.

Hours: Monday–Thursday and Saturday, 10 A.M. to 5 P.M.; Sunday, 1 P.M. to 5 P.M.

Admissions: Small charge for admissions.

For further information write to the Tempe Historical Museum, 809 E. Southern Ave., Tempe, Arizona 85282-5205, or call (602) 350-5100.

Tucson Children's Museum
Tucson, Arizona

Founded in early 1991, the Tucson Children's Museum's mission is to provide a fun and creative environment with hands-on experience for all. Families with children ages 2 to 12 can spend a day at the museum exploring the 12 rooms filled with more than 125 hands-on activities. Theme areas include Rocks and Minerals, The Five Senses, the Cardio-Pulmonary System, Six Simple Machines, Electricity, Self Esteem, Predicting Time, Optics, Careers, Music, Railroads and more.

Several family events, workshops and activities are also sponsored by the museum throughout the year. Four full-time and ten part-time staff members run the museum and the special activities. The 16,000 sq. ft. building is owned by and leased from the City of Tucson.

A happy patron of the Tucson Children's Museum.

Info in brief: Hands-on museum specifically for children and their caregivers.

Location: In the historic Carnegie Library Building on Sixth Avenue.

Hours: (September–May) Tuesday, school tours only; Wednesday–Friday, 9 A.M. to 5 P.M.; Saturday, 10 A.M. to 5 P.M.; Sunday, noon to 5 P.M.; (June–August) Tuesday–Saturday, 10 A.M. to 5 P.M.; Sunday, noon to 5 P.M. (The museum suggests visitors call for exact hours before visiting.)

Admissions: Under 2, free; children, $3; seniors, $4; adults, $5. Every third Sunday is free.

For further information write to the Tucson Children's Museum, 200 S. Sixth Ave., P.O. Box 2609, Tucson, Arizona 85702-2609, or call (520) 792-9985 or FAX (520) 792-0639.

Arkansas

The Children's Museum of Arkansas
Little Rock, Arkansas

For further information contact: The Children's Museum of Arkansas, Union Station, 1400 W. Markham, #200, Little Rock, Arkansas 72201, phone: (501) 374-6655. Member ASTC.

California

Bay Area Discovery Museum
Sausalito, California

The Bay Area Discovery Museum is an indoor/outdoor museum with exhibit centers in seven buildings, an ongoing schedule of workshops and classes, and other programs designed to make learning fun. Families with children 10 years of age and younger are the targeted audience.

The museum opened in its current location in a complex of historic buildings at East Fort Baker, at the northern end of the Golden Gate Bridge in 1991. It was awarded the National Historic Preservation Award in 1992 for its creative use of the facilities. After a couple of expansions, the museum now includes seven buildings with over 20,000 sq. ft. of exhibit space.

Exhibits offered in the galleries include: "San Francisco Bay" (underwater tunnel, a real boat, etc.); "Art Spot" (crafts, art projects, photography); "Architecture and Design"; "Powerhouse" (water power activities); "Discovery Hall" (changing exhibitions); "Science Lab" (with numerous discovery boxes); "Maze of Illusions" (mirrors, holograms and optical illusions); and more. The museum also offers nature walks and classes highlighting the area's indigenous wildlife.

Location: At the northern end of the Golden Gate Bridge on Golden Gate National Recreation Area land.

Hours: (Mid-June–Mid-September) Tuesday–Sunday, 10 A.M. to 5 P.M. (Mid-September–Mid-May) Tuesday–Thursday, 9 A.M. to 4 P.M.; Friday–Sunday, 10 A.M. to 5 P.M. Closed Thanksgiving, Christmas and New Year's Day, Easter and Fourth of July. Open school holidays.

Admissions: Under 1, free; children, $6, adults, $7. Memberships available.

Other sites of interest nearby: The many San Francisco tourist attractions, such as San Francisco Bay.

For further information write to Bay Area Discovery Museum, 557 McReynolds Road, East Fort Baker, Sausalito, California 94965, or call (415) 487-4398.

The Bowers Kidseum
Santa Ana, California

The Bowers Kidseum is an extension of the Bowers Museum of Cultural Art which concentrates on pre–Columbian, Native American, Oceanic, African and Asian art. The Kidseum provides hands-on arts and cultural activities in the same areas for children ages 5 to 12 and their families. The interactive and hands-on exhibits feature masks, instruments, puppets and costumes for dress up from around the world. Little visitors can also go back in time in the Native American "Time Vault" and use grinding stones or learn about early Californians. A hands-on Art Lab offers a range of projects from creating an Asmat drum of New Guinea to designing your own African cloth.

Other special features in the museum include live storytellers on the

The Bowers Kidseum (COURTESY VICTOR BALDWIN)

weekends and ethnic design face painting. Kidseum artists adorn children's faces with traditional designs such as Aboriginal face design, Aztec symbols, Mehndi hand designs from India and more. Family festivals, teacher workshops, art camps and other special events are also offered at various times throughout the year.

Info in brief: Hands-on, interactive museum for children ages 5 to 12 and their caregivers.

Location: Two blocks south of the 5 Freeway.

Hours: Thursday–Friday, 2 P.M. to 5 P.M.; Saturday and Sunday, 10 A.M. to 4 P.M. The museum suggests visitors call ahead of time for a weekly update of scheduled times, prices and events.

Admissions: Under 5, free; children (5–12), $2; students (with ID), $4; adults, $6; seniors, $4. This price also includes same day admission to the Bowers Museum of Cultural Art at 2002 N. Main Street.

Other sites of interest nearby: Bowers Museum of Cultural Art, Discovery Science Center — Launch Pad, Disneyland and other California tourist attractions.

For further information write to The Bowers Kidseum, 1802 N. Main St., Santa Ana, California 92706, or call (714) 480-1520 or FAX (714) 480-0053.

California Science Center
formerly California Museum of Science and Industry
Los Angeles, California

The California Museum of Science and Industry will become the California Science Center at the end of 1997. The new museum will be housed in a bigger building filled with hands-on and Disney-style collections exhibits.

Currently, CMSI is a hands-on, interactive museum for children and their families. Four main gallery areas include the Hall of Health, Technology Hall, Science South and Aerospace Hall. In the new facility, the California Science Center exhibits will be presented in four thematic "worlds": World of Life, Creative World, World of the Pacific, and Worlds Beyond. Phase I (due to open in 1997) will include the World of Life and Creative World with preview exhibits for the other "worlds." The highlight of the World of Life exhibit will be "Body Works," a 50-foot-long, transparent human figure with organ systems that are illuminated by fiber optics. Both "worlds" will have models, presentations, illustrations and hands-on activities. Overall, when completed, the California Science Center will offer state-of-the-art, high-tech exhibits in one of the largest children's museums in the country.

California Science Center

The CMSI IMAX Theater currently offers visitors a five-story screen and surround sound speakers with four, 40-minute films on the schedule. The IMAX will remain an integral part of the new science center.

Info in brief: An interactive, hands-on and technology-filled museum for the entire family. An IMAX Theater is also available.

Location: Exposition Park in Los Angeles.

Hours: Daily, 10 A.M. to 5 P.M. Closed Thanksgiving, Christmas and New Year's Day. IMAX Theater shows and prices are subject to change without notice, so be sure to contact the museum before visiting.

Admissions: (Exhibits) free. (IMAX Theater) under 3, free; children (4–12), $3.75; students (13+ with ID), $4.75; adults (18–59), $6.25; seniors (60+), $4.25. Evening discount is $3.75 per person from 6 P.M. to 9 P.M. Multiple show discounts are available. Member ASTC.

Other sites of interest nearby: Disneyland, Knott's Berry Farm, Universal Studio Tours, and the many other tourist attractions of Los Angeles.

For further information write to the California Science Center, 700 State Dr., Exposition Park, Los Angeles, California 90037, or call (213) 744-7400 or 744-2014 or FAX (213) 744-2240.

Carlsbad Children's Museum
Carlsbad, California

The Carlsbad Children's Museum is a small hands-on museum for children and their families. Permanent displays offered include "Castle Play" (a medieval castle with dress-up and imagination opportunities), "Kids' Marketplace," "Creative Corner" (an art center with changing weekly projects), "Mirror Magic," "Fishin' Boat," "Solar Energy," and "Little People's Corner."

Info in brief: Small hands-on museum especially for young children and their caregivers.

Location: Behind Neimans.

Hours: Tuesday–Thursday, noon to 5 P.M.; Friday and Saturday, 10 A.M. to 5 P.M.; Sunday, noon to 5 P.M. (summer hours — July 1 to September 2) daily, 10 A.M. to 5 P.M.

Admissions: Under 2, free; all others, $3.50.

For further information write to Carlsbad Children's Museum, 300 Carlsbad Village Drive #103, Carlsbad, California 92008, or call (619) 720-0737.

Bubble activities at Carlsbad Children's Museum.

Chico Creek Nature Center
Chico, California

Chico Creek is more of a nature center than a hands-on children's museum, but is included as an entry in this book due to the interactive museum exhibits, the hands-on animal programs, and the exploratory nature hikes that are offered by the center.

Other programs offered at the center include a summertime nature camp, animal adoption program and birthday parties. At the museum itself, interactive exhibits such as "A Walk Through Time" and "Air Aware" are offered at different times throughout the year. Be sure to contact the museum for the current exhibit on display.

Info in brief: A nature center with some activities geared toward children, especially children who love the outdoors and various aspects of nature.

Location: In the Northern Central Valley of California in Bidwell Park.

Hours: Year-round, Tuesday–Sunday, 10 A.M. to 4 P.M.

Admissions: Free to the public. Special programs require special fees.

Unique characteristic: Chico Creek Nature Center is the only facility of its kind between Redding and Sacramento (approximately 200 miles).

Other sites of interest nearby: Bidwell Park (the third largest municipal park in the country with over 3,000 acres of preserves and developed areas) and other attractions offered at California State University in Chico.

For further information write to Chico Creek Nature Center, 1968 E. 8th St., Chico, California 95928, or call (916) 891-4671.

Children's Discovery Museum of San Jose
San Jose, California

As one of the largest facilities of its kind, the Children's Discovery Museum of San Jose offers more than 150 interactive and evolving exhibits and programs throughout the year. The mission of the museum is to place "emphasis on children's need to learn through concrete interactions," through exploration and play.

In 1990, the museum's unique purple gates opened to 42,000 sq. ft. of exhibit and office space designed by Mexico City–based architect Ricardo Legorreta. The exhibits themselves are designed around the intertwined themes of "Community, Connections and Creativity." Some of the exhibits include: "Streets of San Jose," "Step into the Past," "Doodad Dump," "Waterworks," "Early Childhood Resource Center," computer games/activities and more. Special workshops are also offered.

Location: Close to the heart of downtown San Jose near the San Jose McEnery Convention Center and Center for the Performing Arts.

Hours: Sunday, noon to 5 P.M.; Tuesday–Saturday, 10 A.M. to 5 P.M.; Closed — Monday, Thanksgiving and Christmas.

Admissions: Adults, $6; seniors, $5; children (2–18), $4; school groups, $3 @; 2 and under, free. Memberships available. (Ask about Association of Youth Museums privileges.)

Other sites of interest nearby: Other California tourist attractions.

For further information write to Children's Discovery Museum of San Jose, 180 Woz Way, San Jose, California 95110-2780, or call (408) 298-5437 or FAX (408) 298-6826.

Children's Discovery Museum of the Desert
Rancho Mirage, California

For further information contact: Children's Discovery Museum of the Desert, 42-501 Rancho Mirage Lane, Rancho Mirage, California 92270, phone: (619) 346-2980.

The Children's Museum at La Habra
La Habra, California

Established in 1977 in an historic 1923 railroad depot building, The Children's Museum at La Habra now offers a dinosaur fossil dig exhibit, live bees behind glass exhibit, dress-up theater, science demonstrations, mini grocery store, a carousel, model trains, preschool toys and games, workshops, outreach trunks, a changing exhibit gallery, and much more.

Info in brief: Children's museum exclusively for children and their caregivers.

Location: North Orange County.

Hours: Monday–Saturday, 10 A.M. to 5 P.M.; Sunday, 1 P.M. to 5 P.M.

Admissions: $4 per person.

Unique Exhibits: "Operation M.A.C.K." (Museum Accessibility for Challenged Kids); "Puzzles of Places: A Kids Eye View of Geography" (interactive puzzle exhibit).

Other sites of interest nearby: Gene Autry Western Heritage Museum, Southwest Museum (Indians), California Afro-American Museum, Los Angeles Children's Museum (see listing), Los Angeles Zoo, California Museum of Science and Industry, Natural History Museum of Los Angeles County, Disneyland and more. The Children's Museum at La Habra will send an excellent list of "Places to Go with Your Kids" at your request.

For further information write to The Children's Museum at La Habra, 301 S. Euclid St., La Habra, California 90631, or call (310) 905-9693.

Children's Museum of San Diego
Museo de los Niños
San Diego, California

Opened originally in 1981, the museum has been in the works at its present location since 1993. The hands-on museum emphasizes experiences in the arts and humanities and offers programs and exhibits for children, teens and adults. Most exhibitions are designed in cooperation with specific artists.

Both long-term and short-term exhibits are offered along with several permanent displays. One example of a long-term exhibit is "Mi Casa Es Tu Casa/My House Is Your House." This bi-national, state-of-the-art virtual reality installation links children in Mexico City with children in San Diego through a common cyberspace "playhouse." A short-term exhibit, "Mini-City," is an example of contemporary installation art conceptualized by artist

Amanda Farber. In it, visitors create a miniature city using various materials provided. One permanent display designed by artist Alberto Caro is "Culinary Culture" where visitors are encouraged to explore the "roots" of different foods, along with the "roots" of their own families.

Special programs, workshops and events are also offered, with a range from small intimate grouping to large-scale arts performances.

Info in brief: A unique hands-on arts and humanities museum for children of all ages. While some of the permanent exhibits are similar to those found in other children's museums, this museum offers unique arts experiences in uniquely designed exhibit areas.

Location: On the corner of Island Avenue and Front Street in downtown San Diego.

Hours: Tuesday–Sunday, 10 A.M. to 5 P.M.

Admissions: Under 2, free; adults and students, $5; seniors (65+), $3.

Unique exhibitions: Most of the short and long-term exhibits are designed by different artists, who give each exhibit its own unique flair.

Other sites of interest nearby: The San Diego Zoo, the Mexican border and its border towns, and the many tourist attractions in San Diego.

For further information write to Children's Museum of San Diego/Museo de los Niños, 200 W. Island Ave., San Diego, California 92101, or call (619) 233-KIDS or FAX (619) 233-8796.

The Children's Museum of Stockton
Stockton, California

Opened in March 1989, The Children's Museum of Stockton was inspired by the tragic Cleveland School shooting of 1989. Five children were killed and 30 wounded, including one teacher, Janet Geng. Ms. Geng's goal became to offer a safe, violence-free place where children could learn and have fun.

The Allosaurus exhibit at The Children's Museum of Stockton.

The museum's permanent exhibit area, "Mini-City," offers children the chance to work some parts of a real police car, bus and fire engine, plus work in a post office, bank and more. Temporary exhibits are also offered along with visual and performing arts displays. A special area for tiny tots and toddlers is available, as well as special group and family tours.

Info in brief: A hands-on participatory children's museum inspired by the Children's Museum in Washington, D.C.

Location: Downtown Stockton, across the street from the historic waterfront warehouse.

Hours: Tuesday–Saturday, 9 A.M. to 4 P.M.; Sunday, noon to 5 P.M.; closed Monday, New Year's Day, Easter, Thanksgiving and Christmas.

Admissions: Under 2, free; others, $4. Memberships available. Member of the American Youth Museum Network. (All children must be accompanied by an adult.)

Other sites of interest nearby: The Haggin Museum (1201 N. Pershing Ave.) and the World Wildlife Museum & Studio (1245 W. Weber Ave.).

For further information write to The Children's Museum of Stockton, 402 W. Weber Ave., Stockton, California 95203, or call (209) 465-4386 or FAX (209) 465-4394.

Chula Vista Nature Center
Chula Vista, California

The Chula Vista Nature Center is a fully accredited museum which specializes in interactive science exhibits and programs. Its mission is to "serve the public with educational programs and to ensure the preservation of important natural resources."

Approximately four school field trips are scheduled each day. A number of free and fee-based classes are offered along with outreach programs, sleepovers, and nature walks. In 1994, the Gunpowder Point Interpretive Trails opened. This 1.2 mile stroll on the refuge offers visitors opportunities to interact with and learn about the natural ecosystems in the area, especially the Sweetwater Marsh. Inside, modern technology offers opportunities to experience various science phenomenon, films and experiments.

Info in brief: Good combination of nature center and hands-on exhibits of interest to the whole family.

Location: On San Diego Bay approximately 7 miles south of downtown San Diego and 7 miles north of the international border.

Hours: Tuesday–Sunday, 10 A.M. to 5 P.M.; Monday (June, July and August), 10 A.M. to 5 P.M.; closed Thanksgiving and the day after, Christmas Eve and Christmas Day, New Year's Eve and New Year's Day, and Easter Sunday.

Admissions: Adults, $3.50; seniors (65+), $2.50; juniors (6–17), $1; under 6, free (cash only). Memberships available. (Member of American Association of Museums.)

Other sites of interest nearby: San Diego Bay attractions, Pacific Coast beaches, Mexico, San Diego Zoo, and other California attractions.

For further information write to the Chula Vista Nature Center, 100 Gunpowder Point Dr., Chula Vista, California 91910-1201, or call (619) 422-2964 or FAX (619) 422-2964. E-mail: sneudeck@ucsd.edu. Web site: <http://sdcc12.ucsd.edu/(SIGN)wa12/cvnature.html>.

Coyote Point Museum
San Mateo, California

The Coyote Point Museum is an environmental center which offers visitors a multi-sensory overall view of the ecology of the Bay Area in the indoor environmental hall, along with outdoor theme gardens, an 8,000 sq. ft. walk-through songbird aviary, and wildlife habitats. Family members of all ages will enjoy the displays and activities provided. From September to May, the second weekend of each month is designated as "Family Activity Day," with crafts, games, experiments, speakers and storytellers offered to all visitors.

Info in brief: Museum for the general public with designated displays and events of specific interest to children.

Location: Six miles south of San Francisco Airport, just off Highway 101.

Hours: Tuesday–Saturday, 10 A.M. to 5 P.M.; Sunday, noon to 5 P.M.; closed Monday and most major holidays.

Admissions: Under 4, free; children (4–12), $1; seniors (62+), $2; Adults, $3. First Wednesday of each month, free.

Other sites of interest nearby: San Francisco attractions.

For further information write to the Coyote Point Museum for Environmental Education, 1651 Coyote Point Dr., San Mateo, California 94401, or call (415) 342-7755.

The Discovery Center
Central Valley Science Museum
Fresno, California

The Discovery Center is a hands-on children's science museum. Established in 1956, the current 5-acre site now offers both indoor and outdoor scientific exploratory experiences for children of all ages.

Special workshops, events and presentations are also offered to the public, while school groups can ask for a field trip experience or a program from the "Suitcase Science" offerings.

Info in brief: A small hands-on science museum for children and their caregivers.

Hours: Tuesday–Saturday, 10 A.M. to 4 P.M.; Sunday, noon to 4 P.M.

Admissions: Small admissions charge. Memberships available.

Other sites of interest nearby: Winery tours, and other sites of interest in and around Fresno.

For further information write to The Discovery Center, 1944 N. Winery, Fresno, California 93703, or call (209) 251-5533.

A group visiting The Discovery Center at Fresno, California.

Discovery Museum of Orange County
Santa Ana, California

This history-centered discovery museum is an interactive learning environment where visitors can journey back to turn-of-the-century Southern California. Aspects of daily life, such as playing a pump organ, using a hand-cranked telephone, looking through a stereoscope, washing clothes on a scrub board, wearing Victorian clothes, and much more are available for young (and not so young) visitors to experience.

The museum is located in an area known as The Historical Plaza which contains the Kellogg House and three structures from the John Maag ranch (ranch house, carriage house and water tower). The museum is located in the fully-restored Kellogg House, originally built in 1898 and moved to its present site in 1980. An engineer, H. C. Kellogg designed a unique home which is itself a museum highlight. Besides these historical structures, special demonstrations and events are offered throughout the year in and around the plaza. Be sure to contact the museum for exact details and schedules. A 300-bush rose garden and gazebo and several hundred citrus trees are also on the grounds.

The Discovery Museum of Orange County.

Info in brief: An 11-acre site which offers numerous activities, one of which is a hands-on children's historical museum.

Hours (Public Tours): Wednesday–Friday, 1 P.M. to 5 P.M.; Sunday, 11 A.M. to 3 P.M.

Admissions: Children, $2.50; adults, $3.50; seniors, $2.50. Memberships available.

Unique exhibitions: Storybook Teas and Seasonal Teas scheduled well in advance.

Other sites of interest nearby: Disneyland and other Orange County attractions.

For further information write to The Discovery Museum of Orange County, 3101 W. Harvard St., Santa Ana, California 92704, or call (714) 540-0404.

The Exploratorium
San Francisco, California

According to *Newsweek* magazine, "There are two models for great American amusement centers…Disneyland and the Exploratorium. This place feeds all the senses." The Exploratorium itself advertises as a museum of "science, art and human perception," meaning that creative thinking is encouraged as much as the critical thinking encouraged by most other museums.

The Exploratorium is one of the largest children's museums in the nation, with over 650 exhibits on the grounds. The building itself, part of the Palace of Fine Arts designed by architect Bernard Maybeck, is the only survivor of the Panama Pacific Exposition of 1915. Founded in 1969 by physicist Frank Oppenheimer, the museum now features a 50-ft.-high, 103,000 sq. ft. interior which houses permanent and temporary displays and exhibits, classrooms, machine, wood, electronics and welding shops (most open to the public for viewing), the 175-seat McBean Theater, a Life Science laboratory, a reference library/media center, the museum store and a cafe.

Limited space permits only a brief description of the many facets of this museum. Suffice it to say that the goal of the museum is to provide opportunities for learning which are not likely to be experienced elsewhere. The exhibits which encourage this learning fall into 13 broad categories: light, color, sound, music, motion, animal behavior, electricity, heat and temperature, language patterns, hearing, touch, vision, waves and resonance, and weather.

Info in brief: One of the largest (per sq. ft. and per exhibit) hands-on children's museums in the nation.

Location: San Francisco's Marina district.

Hours: (Summer — Memorial Day to Labor Day) open 7 days a week, 10 A.M. to 6 P.M.; Wednesday, 10:00 A.M. to 9:30 P.M. (Winter) Tuesday–Sunday, 10 A.M. to 5 P.M.; Wednesday, 10 A.M. to 9:30 P.M.; closed Monday, except holidays.

Admissions: Fee charged, but no one is denied admission because they cannot pay. Discounts given to seniors, students, groups and the disabled. Memberships available. Member of Association of Youth Museums. Member ASTC.

Unique exhibits: Many.

Other sites of interest nearby: Golden Gate Bridge, Fisherman's Wharf and many other San Francisco attractions.

For further information write to The Exploratorium, 3601 Lyon Street, San Francisco, California 94123, or call (415) 563-7337 or (415) 567-0709 or FAX (415) 561-0307. Internet: lindad*exploratoriun.edu.

Explorit Science Center
Davis, California

Since 1982, Explorit has encouraged the exploration of science, using familiar everyday things as well as the "real stuff" of science. A hands-on open science lab invites children to experiment in various aspects of science, math and technology. Topics change every eight weeks. Permanent exhibits include live reptiles, and a Discovery Den for younger children.

Info in brief: A small hands-on exploratory science museum for children.

Location: 3141 5th Street in East Davis, housed in a ranch-style house, surrounded by expansive lawns and majestic oak trees.

Hours: Tuesday–Friday, 2 P.M. to 4:30 P.M.; Saturday, 11 A.M. to 4:30 P.M.; Sunday, 1 P.M. to 4:30 P.M. Most Monday holidays, open 1 P.M. to 4:30 P.M. Closed other major holidays and during exhibition change weeks. Call ahead for schedule.

Admissions: $3. Members, children under 4, and teachers are admitted free. Fourth Saturday of each month is free admissions for all visitors. Member ASTC.

For further information write to Explorit Science Center, P.O. Box 1288, Davis, California 95617-1288, or call (916) 756-0191 or FAX (916) 756-1227. E-mail: explorit@dcn.davis.ca.us. Website: http://www.dcn.davis.ca.us/GO/EXPLORIT/

Kidspace Museum
Pasadena, California

Kidspace is a hands-on, participatory children's museum targeting children from 2 to 10. Exhibits have been developed in the areas of art, science, music and communication. Exhibit titles include "Eco-Beach," "Vons Mini-Market," "International Mask Gallery," "Critter Caverns," "Mouse House," "KCBS Television Station," "Backstage," "Stargazer Planetarium," "Firestation Kidspace," and "Toddler Territory." Special events and programs are also offered periodically.

The museum is planning a relocation to a new facility at the former Fannie Morrison Center in Brookside Park sometime in 1997 or 1998. (Be sure to contact the museum before visiting.) While the location may change, the focus of educating children through hands-on experiences will remain the same. Hopefully, more exhibits will be built at the new facility.

Info in brief: A hands-on, participatory museum for young children (ages 2–10) and their caregivers.

Location: New location expected in late 1997 or early 1998.

Hours and Admissions: Please contact museum for current scheduling and admissions prices. Member AYM.

For further information write to Kidspace, 390 S. El Molino Ave., Pasadena, California 91101, or call (818) 449-9144.

Lake Arrowhead Children's Museum
Lake Arrowhead, California

The Lake Arrowhead Children's Museum is a hands-on museum with activities geared for children ages 12 and under. Exhibits and programs are designed to encourage learning by doing, imagining, choosing and creating. Opened in 1991, the 2,500 sq. ft. museum currently offers a bubble area, a human habitrail, a Geo Safari learning center, a recycling craft center, a child-sized village, a toddler area, a camping exhibit, a theater/stage area, "Dino Dig," science experiments and a changing exhibits gallery. Special activities are also offered throughout the year.

Info in brief: Hands-on museum especially for children ages 12 and under and their caregivers.

Location: In Lake Arrowhead Village, lower level, at the end of the peninsula right on the shore of Lake Arrowhead.

The Ant Wall at the Lake Arrowhead Children's Museum.

Hours: Summer, everyday from 10 A.M. to 6 P.M.; winter, everyday (except Tuesday) from 10 A.M. to 5 P.M.

Admissions: Under 2, free; ages 2–59, $3.50; seniors (60+), $2.50. Memberships available.

Other sites of interest nearby: Lake Arrowhead and its accompanying tourist attractions.

For further information write to Lake Arrowhead Children's Museum, P.O. Box 321, Lake Arrowhead, California 92352, or call (909) 336-3093 or FAX (909) 336-2173.

Launch Pad
Discovery Science Center
Costa Mesa, California

Launch Pad is the preview facility of Discovery Science Center which is planned to open in 1998 in Santa Ana. The Discovery Science Center will be a 76,000 sq. ft. science learning facility featuring over 100 interactive exhibits emphasizing science, math and technology. A large format theater will also be on the premises. In the meantime, Launch Pad offers visitors 40 hands-on science exhibits for exploration, along with special activities and events, workshops, summer camps and more. At least one major event is offered each month — be sure to contact the museum before visiting.

Location: (Launch Pad) third floor of Crystal Court Shopping Center at South Coast Plaza in Costa Mesa — corner of Bear and Sunflower. DSC will be located on the west side of Main Street at the Santa Ana Freeway.

Hours: Weekdays, 10 A.M. to 7 P.M.; Saturday, 10 A.M. to 7 P.M.; Sunday, 11 A.M. to 6 P.M. Closed Thanksgiving, Christmas, New Year's Day, Easter and July 4.

Admissions (Launch Pad): Children (3–12), $5; adults (13 and over) when accompanying a child, free; adults (when entering alone), $5. Memberships are available. Member of ASTC.

For further information write to The Discovery Science Center–Launch Pad, 3333 Bear St., No. 323, Costa Mesa, California 92626, or call (714) 546-2061 or FAX (714) 546-0949. For information on the Discovery Science Center's progress write to 201 E. Sandpointe, Ste. 320, Santa Ana, California 92707, or call (714) 540-2001.

Lindsay Wildlife Museum
Walnut Creek, California

A museum member with friend
(© THE LINDSAY MUSEUM).

More than 50 species of California wildlife are displayed in an exhibit hall focused on learning to live with and conserve nature. The motto here is "Connecting People and Wildlife." Innovative children's programs, a unique pet library (which allows family members to "check out" pets), a wildlife rehabilitation hospital and a hands-on discovery room for toddlers are offered year-round. Special events and festivals are also held periodically.

Info in brief: A nature center with a hands-on discovery room for very young children.

Location: Larkey Park in Walnut Creek.

Hours: (Summer) Wednesday–Friday, 10 A.M. to 5 P.M.; Saturday and Sunday, 10 A.M. to 5 P.M. (School year) Wednesday–Friday, noon to 5 P.M.; Saturday and Sunday, 10 A.M. to 5 P.M.

Admissions: Under 3, free; children (3–17), $2.50; adults, $4.50; seniors, $3.50. Memberships available. Member ASTC.

Unique attraction: "Pet Library."

For further information write to the Lindsay Wildlife Museum, 1931 First Ave., Walnut Creek, California 94596, or call (510) 935-1978 or FAX (510) 935-8015. Website: www.wildlife-museum.org.

Los Angeles Children's Museum
Los Angeles, California

The Los Angeles Children's Museum uses both directed and non-directed play to extend knowledge that children have hopefully acquired in school or at home. The 15,000 sq. ft. of exhibit space hold 15 interactive exhibits. The main exhibits are "Video Zone," "Club Eco," "Take Care of Yourself," and H_2O, "The Story of Water," "Sticky City," "Shadow Box," and "Art Loft."

From its inception in 1978, the museum has continued its goal of growth

These boys are enjoying one of the interactive exhibits at the Los Angeles Children's Museum (PHOTOGRAPH BY ANDREW COMINS).

and expansion. Its original "temporary headquarters" have now become its "permanent" location (leased from the city of Los Angeles), with building improvements and new exhibits added each year, and paid employees added to the volunteers who still help run the museum. Special workshops and theater productions have also been added to the attractions offered.

Info in brief: Hands-on, participatory museum exclusively for children.

Location: Downtown Los Angeles. Easily accessible by freeway and within walking distance from Union Station.

Hours: (Year-round) Saturday and Sunday, 10 A.M. to 5 P.M.; (summers) Monday–Friday, 11:30 A.M. to 5 P.M. and some holidays. Group reservations also available.

Admissions: Under 2, free; others, $5.

Other sites of interest nearby: Japanese-American National Museum, the Geffen Contemporary Museum and the many other Los Angeles attractions.

For further information write to Los Angeles Children's Museum, 301 N. Main St., Los Angeles, California 90012, or call (213) 687-8800 or 8825.

My Jewish Discovery Place
Los Angeles, California

Since its beginning a few short years ago in 1992, My Jewish Discovery Place has won several awards. Its traveling museum is booked up months in advance and many famous people have experienced its exhibits and programs.

The museum proper is a hands-on museum where visitors are encouraged to learn about Jewish history, tradition, customs, values, holidays, heroes, folklore, music, dance, and drama as well as Shabbat, Israel and Hebrew language. Self-directed learning opportunities have been designed for children 3–11 years of age and their families. More than 20 unique exhibits include "A Walk Back in Time," "Happy Birthday Dear Jerusalem," "People Helping People," "Bendigamos: The Blessings of Sephardic Life," "Discovery Airplane," "Miniature Model Synagogue" and more.

Info in brief: Hands-on, exploratory children's museum.

Location: On the lobby level of the Westside Jewish Community Center of Greater Los Angeles.

Hours: Tuesday–Thursday, 12:30 P.M. to 4 P.M.; Sunday, 12:30 P.M. to 5 P.M. Group tours available by appointment. Closed all national holidays and Jewish holidays.

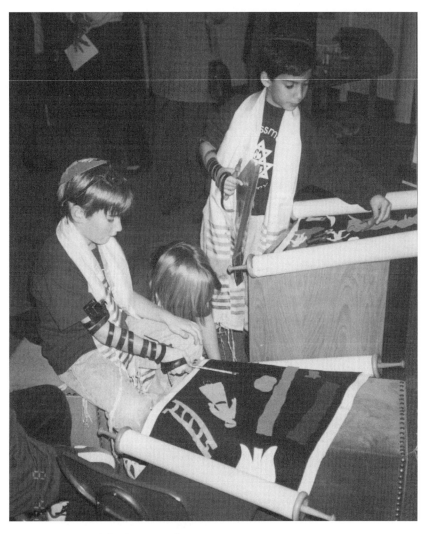

My Jewish Discovery Place (PHOTOGRAPH BY SHERRI KADOVITZ).

Admissions: Under age 2, free; ages 3–7, $2; over 7, $3.

Unique feature: All exhibits focus on Jewish life.

Other sites of interest nearby: The many tourist attractions of Los Angeles.

For further information write to My Jewish Discovery Place of Jewish Community Centers of Great Los Angeles, 5870 W. Olympic Blvd., Los Angeles, California 90036, or call (213) 857-0036. Web site: http://Shamash.nysernet.org.nfjc.jets.html.

Palo Alto Junior Museum & Zoo
Palo Alto, California

The Palo Alto Junior Museum & Zoo is a small children's museum operated by the Department of Community Services in the City of Palo Alto. The museum offers a variety of hands-on educational opportunities which encourage children to touch, look, and listen as they learn by discovery.

Permanent displays include "PlaySpot," an interactive play area for preschoolers and their caregivers; "Starlab," an inflatable planetarium; and the Zoo, located adjacent to the museum. Other temporary exhibits are made available throughout the year. Other educational opportunities offered include classes, workshops, interpretive programs and science outreach programs.

Info in brief: Hands-on, exclusively for children and their caregivers.

Location: 1451 Middlefield Road in Palo Alto, just north of the intersection of Embarcadero Road.

Hours: Tuesday–Saturday, 10 A.M. to 5 P.M.; Sunday, 1 P.M. to 4 P.M.

Admissions: No admissions charge, but donations are appreciated.

Other sites of interest nearby: Museums in Palo Alto and other California tourist attractions.

For further information write to the Palo Alto Junior Museum & Zoo, City of Palo Alto, Dept. of Community Services, 1451 Middlefield Road, Palo Alto, California 94301, or call (415) 329-2111.

The Randall Museum
San Francisco, California

The Randall Museum is not always open to the public for self-guided tours. It is considered to be an educational, program-based museum featuring arts, science and live animal exhibits for all ages. School and group field trips, after-school programs, evening and Saturday classes, and camps are their top priority. You should contact the museum before visiting, because, even though museum hours are given, it appears that most activities are done in groups. Many new changes are in the works at the time of this publication, however, so open public visitation hours may soon be available.

The Randall Museum currently houses changing exhibits, a live animal collection, woodworking shop, ceramics room, darkroom, lapidary workshop, and an art room. An auditorium and several classrooms are also available along with picnic facilities outside.

Info in brief: An educational, program-based museum apparently open for groups only.

Location: Corona Heights Park.

Hours: Tuesday–Saturday, 10 A.M. to 5 P.M.; animal room hours, 10:30 A.M. to 1 P.M. and 2 P.M. to 5 P.M.; model train hours, 2nd and 4th Saturday of each month, 1 P.M. to 5 P.M.

Admissions: No admissions fees charged; small charge for some events and classes.

Other sites of interest nearby: Golden Gate Park, Buena Vista Park, and other San Francisco tourist attractions.

For further information write to The Randall Museum, 199 Museum Way, San Francisco, California 94114, or call (415) 554-9600.

Reuben H. Fleet Space Theater and Science Center
San Diego, California

The Space Theater and Science Center is operated by the San Diego Space and Science Foundation. Programs are offered in two main areas — the Space Theater and the Science Center. In the Space Theater, visitors can experience an Omnimax film or planetarium program. (In fact, the term Omnimax was coined by the Space Theater founders for the giant tilted dome screen and fish-eye effect created by the projection of the new IMAX films onto their tilted dome screen.) In the Science Center, more than 60 interactive exhibits allow visitors to experience science.

Conceived in 1957, the museum opened on a small scale with a unique model planetarium in 1965. This area now offers both planetarium and Omnimax Theater presentations. The Science Center facility opened to the public in 1973. The newest permanent exhibition, "Signals," teaches about how signals are processed to deliver information. Visitors can send messages to a partner or play with video phones, sound tubes and digital computers, or become a FAX machine. Besides these and the other 50-plus permanent exhibits, several traveling exhibits, special programs and special events are offered throughout the year.

Info in brief: A hands-on museum for children, plus a planetarium/Omnimax Theater.

Location: On the Prado in Balboa Park, two blocks south of the San Diego Zoo on Park Blvd.

Hours: Daily, open at 9:30 A.M. Contact the museum for daily schedule and closing times.

Admissions: (Space Theater) under 5, free; juniors (5–15), $3.50; adults, $6.50; seniors (65+), $5. Special prices are in effect when more than one film is showing. (Science Center only) under 5, free; juniors, $1.25; adults and seniors, $2.50. Admission to the Science Center is $1 for adults and seniors and $.50 for juniors with purchase of Space Theater ticket. Member ASTC.

Other sites of interest nearby: San Diego Zoo and other San Diego tourist attractions.

For further information write to the Reuben H. Fleet Space Theater and Science Center, Balboa Park, P.O. Box 33303, San Diego, California 92163-3303, or call (619) 238-1233 (TDD 238-2480) or 232-6866 or FAX (619) 231-8971. Website: www.rhfleet.org.

The Watts Towers of Simon Rodia
Watts Towers Arts Center
Los Angeles, California

Created by an immigrant Italian tile laborer known as Sam Rodia, the Watts Towers are a group of nine multi-media structures (mostly iron, cement and tile) which have been part of the Watts skyline (and culture) since the 1920s. Starting in 1921, Rodia worked on the towers until 1954 at which time he simply moved on, endeavoring to put that part of his life behind him. Until his death in 1965, Rodia had very little else to do with the Towers.

In 1958 a committee of interested parties was formed to preserve Rodia's work and make it a cultural center for the community. From its beginning, the center has offered free informal art classes with an emphasis on developing interest in the arts among children.

The center's first classes met outdoors on the foundation of Rodia's house, then in an abandoned building next door. The Watts Towers Arts Center now is housed in a 2,000 sq. ft. facility which boasts of having "some of the most successful art programs in the city." Permanent exhibits housed in the facility now include the "Folk Instrument Gallery" and an African Sculpture collection. The main gallery offers changing exhibitions of contemporary art by local and national artists. The center also sponsors the Simon Rodia Watts Towers Jazz Festival and the "Day of the Drum Festival" each September.

The Watts Towers are listed on the National Register of Historic Places, are a National Historic Landmark, a State of California Historic Monument, a State of California Historic Park and are designated as Historic-Cultural Monument No. 15 by the City of Los Angeles Cultural Heritage Commission. The tallest tower is 99½ feet high and has the longest slender reinforced concrete column in the world.

Although not an exclusive children's museum, the Center does pride itself in providing an outlet for creative young artists and offers a "Visiting Schools" and "Neighboring Schools Program" to area schools, along with the wonder of the Towers themselves.

Info in brief: The Center provides cultural enrichment programs — tours, lectures, changing exhibits and studio workshops for both teachers and school-age children.

Location: 1765 East 107th Street, Los Angeles.

Hours: Be sure to contact the Center before visiting as hours change according to events scheduled.

Admissions: All workshops and events are free to the public.

Unique exhibits or exhibitions: The "Towers," "The Folk Instrument Gallery," African Sculpture collection, music festivals described above.

Other sites of interest nearby: Tourist attractions of Greater Los Angeles and the surrounding areas.

For further information write to Watts Towers Arts Center, 1727 E. 107th Street, Los Angeles, California 90002, or call (213) 485-1795 or FAX (213) 564-7030.

World Wildlife Museum
Stockton, California

The World Wildlife Museum is not a hands-on museum. It is a natural history museum with close to 3,000 mounted zoological specimens representing wildlife from all seven continents of the world. In fact, it has the largest, most complete collection of mounted zoological specimens in the world.

The main goal of the museum is to educate children as to the plight of wildlife and to convince them of the importance of the individual's role and responsibility in maintaining a sensible balance of nature. Exhibits introducing children to specimens of nature in life-like settings which they may never have seen before include Sheep Mountain, African Water Hole, Waterfall/Rainforest, Nile Crocodile/Sable Antelope, Lions/Zebras, Alaska Brown Bear, Deer of the World and Great White Shark. Special events and guided tours are also offered.

Info in brief: A natural history museum which contains the world's most complete collection of mounted zoological specimens in life-like settings.

Mounted specimens in the World Wildlife Museum

Location: Waterfront, downtown Stockton.

Hours: Wednesday–Sunday, 9 A.M. to 5 P.M.

Admissions: Under 3, free; children (3–16), $3; seniors (60+), $3; adults, $4.

Unique exhibits: World's largest mounted zoological collection.

Other sites of interest nearby: Children's Museum, Hagin Museum, Mickey Grove Zoo and Museum.

For further information write to World Wildlife Museum, 1245 W. Weber Ave., Stockton, California 95203, or call (209) 465-2834 or FAX (209) 941-4430.

Youth Science Center
Hacienda Heights, California

The Youth Science Center was established in Fullerton, California, in 1962 and has now opened branches in Hacienda Heights (1984) and Pico Rivera (1992). Besides the many exhibits, classes, lectures, and field trips are offered with an aim to increase children's interest in science and to increase their appreciation and respect for the environment. Visitors can experiment with exhibits involving volcanoes, astronomy, weather, the body, insects, reptiles and liquid crystals. Several MacIntosh computers with CD-ROM drives are also available for use, and a StarLab portable planetarium was added in 1993.

Currently, 24 instructors offer classes at various times throughout the year. Five of these 24 have been honored as "Teacher of the Year" or "Teacher of the Month" in their districts. Even though the main emphasis is placed on school groups, the museum is open to the public three days a week during the school year. Summer hours allow visitors to visit five days of the week.

Info in brief: A small hands-on children's museum with a target audience of elementary school-aged children.

Location: Wedgeworth Elementary School on Wedgeworth Drive in Hacienda Heights.

Hours: (School year) Wednesday and Friday, 1 P.M. to 4 P.M.; Saturday, 10 A.M. to 2 P.M.; (summer) Monday–Friday, 8:30 A.M. to 12 P.M. Be sure to contact museum for special Saturday science classes times and other program information.

Admissions: Free (donations accepted).

Other sites of interest nearby: Hsi Lai Buddhist Temple (largest Buddhist temple in North America), La Habra Children's Museum, Knott's Berry Farm (Buena Park) and other California tourist attractions.

For further information write to Youth Science Center, 16949 Wedgeworth Dr., Hacienda Heights, California 91745, or call (818) 854-9825.

Colorado

The Children's Museum of Denver
Denver, Colorado

Since 1973, the Children's Museum of Denver has offered innovative, hands-on exhibits, educational programs, theater performances and special events encouraging children "to explore, create, discover and imagine themselves in the world around them." The targeted audience is children ages 2 to 12 and their families. Permanent exhibits include: DiscoveryLabs (ScienceLab, CompuLab, and StormCenter 4); We All Live Downsteam; KidSlope, an outdoor slope that operates year-round; KidSkate, in-line skating; SizeWise, basketball-theme area; SpokesPeople, wheelchair-theme area; Play Partners, role-play area; and The Grocery Store. Other temporary exhibits, including a portable, inflatable planetarium, are offered throughout the year. Special workshops, classes and shows are also offered.

Info in brief: Hands-on museum for children ages 2 to 12 and their caregivers.

Location: I-25 and 23rd Ave.

Hours: Tuesday–Sunday, 10 A.M. to 5 P.M.; open Monday, June–August only; toddler hours, Tuesday and Thursday, 9 A.M. to 10 A.M.

Admissions: Under 1, free; toddlers (1 and 2), $2; others (3–59), $5; seniors (60+), $3. Admissions may vary for special exhibits and events. Memberships are available.

Other sites of interest nearby: The Colorado Railroad Museum, Forney Transportation Museum, Rio Grande Ski Train, Elitch Gardens theme park, skiing attractions and other Denver tourist attractions.

For further information write to The Children's Museum of Denver, 2121 Children's Museum Dr., Denver, Colorado 80211, or call (303) 433-7444 or FAX 433-9520.

Discovery Center Science Museum
Fort Collins, Colorado

For further information contact: Discovery Center Science Museum, 703 E. Prospect, Fort Collins, Colorado 80525, phone: (303) 493-2182. Member ASTC.

DooZoo
Grand Junction, Colorado

The DooZoo Children's Museum began in 1984 as an indoor play space for young children and has developed into a multi-leveled service organization serving families with children of all ages through various programs. Around 8,500 sq. ft. of hands-on, interactive exhibits are offered in the DooZoo, including creative role playing settings, science-oriented displays and demonstrations, changing arts and crafts projects, motor skill development stations and more. All exhibits are designed to encourage parent-child interaction and spark the imagination of children up to 12 years of age and their parents.

Other aspects of this organization include publication of the *Western Colorado Parent Magazine*, the Adventures in Science Enrichment programs for schools, and the Family Theatre Company and Performing Arts Academy.

Info in brief: The DooZoo itself is a hands-on, interactive museum for children and their caregivers.

Admissions: A small admissions fee is charged.

For further information write to the DooZoo Children's Museum, 635 Main, Grand Junction, Colorado 81501, or call (970) 241-5225.

University of Colorado Museum
Boulder, Colorado

The University of Colorado Museum is a natural history museum for people of all ages. Inside the Museum, however, is a hands-on "Discovery Corner" for kids. In the "Discovery Corner" children can try on a turtle shell, weave on a Navajo loom, piece together a buffalo skeleton, view dinosaur remains, and more. An annual "Museum in the Dark" program is also offered for children and their families, along with many special events, changing traveling exhibits, lectures and trips.

Info in brief: An adult museum with one section specifically designated as a hands-on museum for children.

Location: On the Boulder campus in the Henderson Building at 15th and Broadway.

Hours: Monday–Friday, 9 A.M. to 5 P.M.; Saturday, 9 A.M. to 4 P.M.; Sunday, 10 A.M. to 4 P.M. Closed holidays.

Admissions: No admissions fee. Be sure to contact the museum about parking space and fees before visiting.

For further information write to the University of Colorado Museum, Campus Box 218, Boulder, Colorado 80309-0218, or call (303) 492-6892.

Connecticut

Lutz Children's Museum
Manchester, Connecticut

Advertised as the "Everchanging Lutz Children's Museum," this museum offers children the opportunity to explore their world through both hands-on participatory exhibits and special display-type exhibits, both inside and outside. Live animal exhibits change frequently as Lutz rehabilitates orphaned and injured animals and then releases them back into their own environment whenever possible.

Hands-on exhibits change frequently, and such activities as Legomania, marble works, puppets, and weaving are offered. The museum also offers teaching, tours and lectures for school groups as well as kits for teachers to rent.

Info in brief: Hands-on activities, nature walks, live animal exhibits and visual displays for children and adults.

Location: Downtown Manchester, Connecticut (Exit 3 off I-384).

Hours: Tuesday and Wednesday, 2 P.M. to 5 P.M.; Thursday and Friday, 9:30 A.M. to 5 P.M.; Saturday and Sunday, noon to 5 P.M. Closed Mondays and major holidays.

Admissions: Adults, $3; children, $2.50. Memberships are offered.

Unique exhibits or exhibitions: An Alaskan Brown Bear, and an area where children can display their own collections.

For further information write to Lutz Children's Museum, 247 South Main Street, Manchester, Connecticut 06040, or call (860) 643-0949.

The Maritime Aquarium of Norwalk
Norwalk, Connecticut

The Maritime Aquarium consists of the Aquarium area, an IMAX Theater and Maritime Hall. A five-year, $20 million multi-phase expansion is being planned — the first phase being an Environmental Education Center which is scheduled to open in 1998.

The aquarium area of the museum features 20 habitats stocked with more than 125 species indigenous to the Long Island Sound. The entire Aquarium is one of a few in the country solely devoted to one body of water. In Falconer Hall, where the aquarium begins and ends, harbor seals live in a special indoor-outdoor tank, where visitors can watch them being fed three times daily. Several videos and a touch tank are also offered here.

The IMAX Theater at the Maritime Aquarium is the only IMAX Theater in Connecticut. (IMAX is short for "Image MAXimum.") More than two dozen films focusing on natural history and science have been offered here. Film titles change frequently, so it is best to contact the aquarium for current titles before visiting.

The Maritime Hall is a two-story building which features a new series of hands-on displays explaining what a fish is and how it works. A new Shark Touch Pool is also available for visitors to experience (see photograph on front cover of this book). Interactive displays also provide activities which teach about navigational procedures and boatbuilding.

Info in brief: An aquarium, IMAX theater and hands-on children's science center of interest to the whole family.

Location: A few minutes off I-95, at Exit 14 northbound and Exit 15 southbound.

Hours: Daily, 10 A.M. to 5 P.M.; open until 6 P.M. July 1–Labor Day. Closed Thanksgiving and Christmas Day.

Admissions: General admission (aquarium and special exhibits), under 2, free; children (2–12), $6.50; adults, $7.75; seniors (62+), $7.00. IMAX Theater admission, under 2, free; children, $4.75; adults, $6.50; seniors, $5.50. Combination (aquarium and IMAX), children, $9.50; adults, $12; seniors, $10.50. Member ASTC.

Unique exhibitions: All exhibits, touch tanks, etc. focus on species indigenous to the Sound.

Other sites of interest nearby: Essex Steam Train & Riverboat Ride, Valley Railroad Company, The Connecticut Valley Line (Essex); Railroad Museum of New England (Essex); Lake Compounce Amusement Park (Bristol), and Quassy Amusement Park (Middlebury).

For further information write to The Maritime Aquarium at Norwalk, 10 N. Water St., Norwalk, Connecticut 06854, or call (203) 852-0700 or FAX (203) 838-5416.

The New Britain Youth Museum & New Britain Youth Museum Hungerford Park
Kensington, Connecticut

The Greater New Britain Arts Alliance has as its purpose to "work towards creating opportunities for participation in the arts; to provide artistic nourishment to the population, the artists and the arts; and to develop an atmosphere of community support that the arts need and deserve." Member organizations coordinate arts and activities, disseminate information about each other's activities and support and encourage one another through various events and activities. Two members of this unique alliance include the New Britain Youth Museum (a hands-on children's museum) and the New Britain Youth Museum Hungerford Park (a family exploratory nature center).

The Youth Museum, founded in 1956, encourages children and their families to explore the cultures and history of Connecticut and the world. Visual and tactile exhibits are available, with both permanent and changing exhibits on display at various times. The main exhibits include a puppet theater, construction toys, games and a changing activities area. School programs are also offered, both in-house and as an outreach.

The Hungerford Park nature center offers children and their families opportunities to explore their natural environment. Petting zoos, live exotic animals and reptiles and other types of wildlife are available for up close and personal observation. An indoor exhibition area also offers the visitor educational experiences.

Info in brief: The Youth Museum is a hands-on, participatory museum especially for children and their caregivers. The Hungerford Park site is a hands-on nature center.

Hours: (Youth Museum) Tuesday–Friday, 1 P.M. to 5 P.M.; Saturday, 10 A.M. to 4 P.M.; summer, Monday–Friday, 1 P.M. to 5 P.M. (Hungerford Park) Tuesday–Friday, 1 P.M.to 5 P.M.; summer, 11 A.M. to 5 P.M.; Saturday, 10 A.M. to 5 P.M.

Admissions: Youth Museum, free. Hungerford Park, under 2, free; children $1; seniors, $1.50; Adults, $2.

Other sites of interest nearby: New Britain Industrial Museum, New Britain Museum of American Art, New Britain Chorale, Musical Club, Opera, Symphony, Hole in the Wall Theater, and the Repertory Theater of New Britain.

For further information write to The New Britain Youth Museum, 30 High Street, New Britain, Connecticut 06051, or call (860) 225-3020. For Hungerford Park write to The New Britain Youth Museum at Hungerford Park, 191 Farmington Ave., Kensington, Connecticut 06037, or call (860) 827-9064.

Washington, D.C.

Capital Children's Museum
Washington, D.C.

Occupying an entire square block in downtown Washington, D.C., the Capital Children's Museum is a general hands-on children's museum offering exhibits in the arts, sciences, humanities and technology. The goal of the museum is to foster "children's love of learning by encouraging exploration, creativity, imagination, expression and discovery" (brochure).

Opening in 1977 in the Lovejoy Elementary School, the museum is now permanently housed in a former convent that was built in 1873. Current exhibit areas include "Animation," "Mexico," "The City," "Communication," and "Thailand." Each exhibit area offers a multitude of hands-on experiences including giving a puppet show, using a printing press, making a tortilla,

The Chuck Jones Animation Exhibit at Capital Children's Museum.

grinding chocolate, using Morse code, sliding down a fire pole and more. School tours, internships, changing weekend activities, a preschool program, dropout prevention program, special exhibits and animation classes are also offered. (Options Public Charter School is on the grounds.)

Info in brief: Hands-on participatory children's museum.

Location: Downtown Washington, D.C., right behind Union Station.

Hours: Daily, 10 A.M. to 5 P.M.; closed Christmas, New Year's and Thanksgiving Day.

Admissions: Under 2, free; seniors, $4; all other, $6. Memberships available.

Other sites of interest nearby: The many tourist attractions in Washington, D.C.

For further information write to Capital Children's Museum (CCM), 800 Third Street, NE, Washington, D.C. 20002, or call (202) 675-4120 (general info.) or (202) 675-4125 (special activities hotline).

National Postal Museum
Smithsonian Institution
Washington, D.C.

The National Philatelic Collection was established in 1886 at the Smithsonian with one sheet of 10-cent Confederate stamps. The collection now contains more than 16 million items. The National Postal Museum is located on the lower level of the historic City Post Office Building, constructed in 1914. The museum occupies 75,000 sq. ft., with over 23,000 sq. ft. dedicated to exhibition space.

Exhibits include more than displays of stamps. Six exhibit galleries tell the history of postal service in America through interactive and child-oriented displays. A "Self-Guided Tour for Very Young Visitors" brochure is given to children upon entering the museum. This guide directs children to find specific items in the galleries. The Discovery Center, also located in the building, offers daily activities and projects for children and adults.

Docent Ronald Bland leads a school group through the National Postal Museum
(COURTESY SMITHSONIAN INSTITUTION, NATIONAL POSTAL MUSEUM).

Info in brief: While the main emphasis of the museum is visual displays, activities are provided to keep up the child's interest, through interactive displays and child-oriented activities. The Discovery Center is of specific interest to children.

Location: Downtown Washington, D. C.

Hours: 7 days a week, 10 A.M. to 5:30 P.M. Closed Christmas Day.

Admissions: Free

Other sites of interest nearby: The many, many tourist attractions in Washington, D. C., and the surrounding areas, many of which are also free.

For further information write to the National Postal Museum, Smithsonian Institution, 2 Massachusetts Ave., N.E., Washington, D. C. 20560, or call (202) 357-2700 or (202) 357-1729 (TTY for the hearing impaired) or (202) 357-2020 or (202) 357-2991 (tour info).

Rock Creek Nature Center & Planetarium
Rock Creek Park
Washington, D.C.

Rock Creek Park is administered by the National Park Service and offers visitors many activities, including picnicking, playgrounds, tennis, trails, and biking. The park administration also oversees the "Old Stone House" historic site, "Pierce Mill" historic site and the Rock Creek Park Nature Center & Planetarium.

At the Nature Center, planetarium shows are scheduled one or two times each day and young visitors may explore the Nature Discovery Room. This room is designed with games and art supplies to encourage learning about the environment. Visitors must ask the ranger for information about access to this room.

Info in brief: A Nature Center with one small area devoted to hands-on activities for children and their caregivers.

Location: 5200 Glover Road, NW, Washington.

Hours: Wednesday–Sunday, 9 A.M. to 5 P.M. Closed on all federal holidays.

Admissions: Free. (There are some charges for activities in the park, but the nature center is free.)

Other sites of interest nearby: The many tourist attractions of Washington, D.C.

For further information write to Rock Creek Park Nature Center & Planetarium, 5200 Glover Road, NW, Washington, D.C. 20015, or Rock Creek Park, 3545 Williamsburg Lane, N.W., Washington, D.C. 20008-1207, or call (202) 426-6829. Website: http://www.nps.gov/rocr.

Florida

The Bailey-Matthews Shell Museum
Sanibel Island, Florida

The Bailey-Matthews Shell Museum is the only museum in the United States which is devoted solely to shells. More than just a "display" museum, the museum offers the visitor opportunities to increase his scientific knowledge of shells and to learn about the relationship between shells and the web of life.

The museum hosts the second largest library in Florida (in this scientific field) and conducts lectures and seminars throughout the year. Touch Tables are available for children along with special paper "games" that children can play as they tour the exhibits.

Info in brief: Although this museum is not specifically for children, the Touch Tables and impressive displays offer a unique opportunity for children to learn about something that is for most of them fascinating.

Hours: Tuesday–Sunday, 10 A.M. to 4 P.M.

Admissions: Under 7, free; youth (7–17 yrs.), $3; adults, $5.

Unique exhibits: Over 200 species of shells.

Other sites of interest nearby: Thomas Edison and Henry Ford homes, Imaginarium children's museum, Gulf Coast beaches.

For further information write to The Bailey-Matthews Shell Museum, P.O. Box 1580, Sanibel, Florida 33957, or call (941) 395-2233 or FAX (941) 395-6706. Website: www.coconet.com.

The Brevard Museum, Inc.
Cocoa, Florida

The Brevard Museum employs two full-time and four part-time staff who, along with the more than 100 volunteers, help to keep the programs and exhibits running smoothly. More than 12,000 sq. ft. of floor space is devoted to permanent exhibits in ornithology, paleontology, marine biology, archaeology, geology, the Spanish Period, Seminole Indians and pioneer history. A 22-acre nature center is also on the grounds.

Both interpretive and hands-on exhibits are available, with a special "Discovery Room" (all hands-on activities) offered especially for kindergartners through third graders. Puppet shows and a walking tour of historic Cocoa Village are also of special interest to children.

Info in brief: Interpretive museum of interest to the entire family, but with a number of hands-on displays specifically for children.

Hours: Contact museum for specific seasonal hours.

Admissions: Small admissions charge.

Unique exhibitions: The entire museum concentrates on Florida history, culture, and flora and fauna.

Other sites of interest nearby: Numerous Florida tourist attractions, such as Kennedy Space Center.

For further information write to the Brevard Museum, Inc., 2201 Michigan Ave., Cocoa, Florida, 32926, or call (407) 632-1830.

The Children's Science Center
Cape Coral, Florida

The Children's Science Center in Cape Coral is a hands-on exploratory science museum and outdoor nature trail. Science and technology areas explored include holograms, optical illusions, electricity, space, mazes, Calusa Indian technology, fossils and dinosaurs, bubbles, telescope viewing (January–April), bug hunting and more.

Info in brief: Hands-on exploratory museum for children, even on the nature trail.

Location: 2915 NE Pine Island Road.

Hours: Weekdays, 9:30 A.M. to 4:30 P.M.; weekends, noon to 5 P.M.

Admissions: Under 2, free; children (3–16) $2; adults, $4. Member ASTC.

Unique exhibits: Outdoor exploratory nature trail.

Other sites of interest nearby: Calusa Nature Center and Planetarium, Sun Splash Family Waterpark, Six Mile Cypress Slough Preserve, Marine Science Center, Corkscrew Swamp Sanctuary, Thomas Edison and Ford homes (Ft. Myers), Florida beaches.

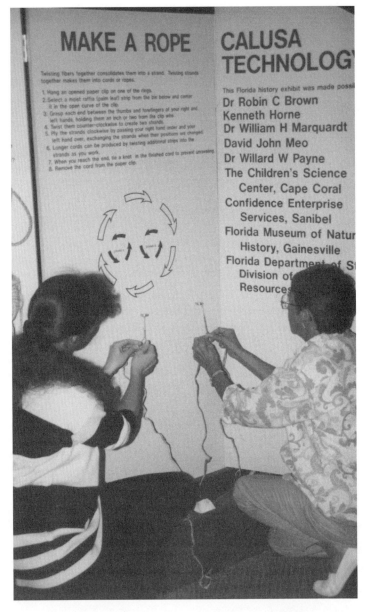

MAKE A ROPE

Twisting fibers together consolidates them into a strand. Twisting strands together makes them into cords or ropes.

1. Hang an opened paper clip on one of the rings.
2. Select a moist raffia (palm leaf) strip from the bin below and center it in the open curve of the clip.
3. Grasp each end between the thumbs and forefingers of your right and left hands, holding them an inch or two from the clip wire.
4. Twist them counter-clockwise to create two strands.
5. Ply the strands clockwise by passing your right hand under and your left hand over, exchanging the strands when their positions are changed.
6. Longer cords can be produced by twisting additional strips into the strands as you work.
7. When you reach the end, tie a knot in the finished cord to prevent unraveling.
8. Remove the cord from the paper clip.

CALUSA TECHNOLOG

This Florida history exhibit was made possi

Dr Robin C Brown
Kenneth Horne
Dr William H Marquardt
David John Meo
Dr Willard W Payne
The Children's Science Center, Cape Coral
Confidence Enterprise Services, Sanibel
Florida Museum of Natur History, Gainesville
Florida Department of S Division of Resource

The Children's Science Center in Cape Coral, Florida.

For further information write to The Children's Science Center, P.O. Box 151381, Cape Coral, Florida 33993, or call (941) 997-0012 or FAX (941) 997-7215.

52   Florida

Explorations V
Polk County's Children's Museum
Lakeland, Florida

Polk County's Children's Museum is a hands-on museum where visitors can pilot a space shuttle, pretend shop at a grocery store, make news at a miniature TV station, learn about banking and more at the permanent exhibits. Rotating exhibits and creative workshops are also offered.

Info in brief: Hands-on, participatory museum for children.

Location: Downtown historic Lakeland, Florida.

Hours: Monday and Tuesday, 9 A.M. to 1 P.M.; Wednesday–Saturday, 9 A.M. to 4 P.M.; Sunday, 1 P.M. to 4 P.M.

Admissions: Small admissions charge.

Other sites of interest nearby: Cypress Gardens, other Florida attractions within an hour's drive.

For further information write to Explorations V Children's Museum, 125 S. Kentucky Ave., Lakeland, Florida 33801, or call (941) 687-3869 or FAX (941) 680-2357.

Children and adults play in the "Once Upon a Time" storybook cottage at Explorations V.

Fantasy of Flight
Polk City, Florida

Opened in 1995, Fantasy of Flight is an aviation-theme attraction featuring more than 20 vintage aircraft, a full-scale realistic diorama of a WWII bombing mission aboard a B-17 Flying Fortress, and flight simulator experiences. The aircraft are a part of the largest private collection of vintage aircraft in the world, belonging to founder Kermit Weeks. The "History of Flight" chronicles air travel from the beginnings of man's attempts at flight to the jet era in realistic displays.

The 300-acre site also houses two private grass runways, a seaplane base and support facilities, hangars used for restoration, maintenance and storage, a gift shop and an Art Deco–style restaurant.

Info in brief: Unique access to flight simulators, not available at many other locations.

Location: 10 miles northeast of Lakeland, Florida, off I-4 (Exit 21); 20 minutes southwest of Walt Disney World.

Hours: Open 365 days a year from 9 A.M. to 5 P.M. Extended hours apply during peak tourist seasons, so be sure to contact Fantasy of Flight before visiting.

Admissions: Under 4, free; children (5–12), $7.95; seniors (60+), $9.95; adults (13–59), $10.95. General admission includes Fantasy of Flight's theme flight experiences and exhibits, but does not include Fightertown flight simulator experience—$5.95 additional cost. Annual Flight Passes are available for $39.95. Parking is free.

Unique exhibits: Flight simulators, vintage aircraft.

Other sites of interest nearby: All the Orlando/Kissimmee/St. Cloud attractions.

For further information write to Fantasy of Flight, P.O. Box 1200, Polk City, Florida 33868-1200, or call (941) 984-3500 or FAX (941) 984-9506. E-mail: rcaborn@4dmg.net (Rod Caborn, Public Relations, Gilbert & Manjura Marketing).

Florida Adventure Museum
Punta Gorda, Florida

For further information contact: Florida Adventure Museum, 260 W. Retta Esplanade, Punta Gorda, Florida 33950, phone: (941) 639-3777. Member ASTC.

Imaginarium
Fort Myers, Florida

Opened in July 1995, the Imaginarium is an interactive, hands-on learning center emphasizing science, the humanities and the uniqueness of the surrounding geographical region. Plans are to build the museum in three phases. Phase I is the hands-on exhibit area currently running. Phase II (opening 1997) is the aquariums of the Gulf of Mexico and regional habitat exhibits. Phase III will include a one-acre, walk-through recreation of an Everglades wetland.

Current facilities include a 12,000 sq. ft. area dedicated to a variety of indoor and outdoor hands-on exhibits in science. More than 13 theme exhibit areas are currently offered to visitors. Eventually a pre-school area and an historical interpretation area will be added. A 150-seat full surround sound system theater offers various programs. A 1,000 sq. ft. programming area (the "Dr. James A. Adams Orientation Center") hosts exhibits, programs and special events. "The Imagination Station" is a 460 sq. ft. area which houses various self-directed activities, art classes, parties and special events. The Museum Store and a 1,300 sq. ft. pavilion area complete the services now available.

Info in brief: A hands-on, interactive children's museum which will also soon house several aquariums.

Location: Built on the site of the Fort Myers Water Treatment Plant at the corner of Cranford Avenue and Martin Luther King, Jr. Boulevard in downtown Fort Myers.

Hours: Monday–Saturday, 10 A.M. to 5 P.M.; Sunday, noon to 5 P.M. Open every day but Christmas and Thanksgiving.

Admissions: Under 3, free; children (3–12), $3; adults (13+), $6. All children must be accompanied by an adult.

Other sites of interest nearby: Thomas Edison's Home, Henry Ford's Winter Home, Fort Myers beaches and other South Florida attractions.

Junior Museum of Bay County
Panama City, Florida

The Junior Museum of Bay County, established in 1967, is a hands-on, interactive museum focusing on science, history and culture. Permanent exhibits include the Natural Trail (through a hardwood swamp), Once Upon a Time (history exhibit), Imagine Me Room (theater), Engine 904 (real engine), Pioneer Homestead (authentic buildings), Discovery Depot (for

toddlers), Body Works, Nature Corner and Hands On Science. Other temporary and or rotating exhibits are put on display in the museum building itself
several times each year.

Info in brief: A village museum and a children's hands-on interactive museum
on the same grounds.

Location: 1731 Jenks Avenue, approximately five minutes from Panama City
Mall.

Hours: Monday–Friday, 9 A.M. to 4:30 P.M.; Saturday, 10 A.M. to 4 P.M.

Other sites of interest nearby: Gulf Coast beaches and the Miracle Strip
amusement park.

For further information write to The Junior Museum of Bay County, 1731
Jenks Ave., Panama City, Florida 32405, or call (904) 769-6128.

Miami Youth Museum
Miami, Florida

The Miami Youth Museum is the oldest children's museum in Florida and
the largest in South Florida. Currently housed in the Paseos (formerly Miracle Center) Mall, plans call for a relocation in 1999 to a new facility. Once built,
the new 50,000 sq. ft. facility will become one of the ten largest children's
museums in the country. The name will be changed at that time to the Miami
Children's Museum. The new facility will be located approximately 2.4 miles
from the present building, but will most likely keep the same phone number.

The Miami Youth Museum is a strictly hands-on, exploratory museum
where children can discover the fun and facts about real-life roles through permanent and changing special interactive exhibits. A few of the exhibits include
playing at becoming a police officer, fire fighter, or other uniformed worker,
driving a child-sized model of a Metro-Dade police car or fire truck, shopping at a Publix Supermarket, visiting a dentist's office, starring in the NBC-6
Newsroom news, and more. Special workshops and classes are also offered.

Info in brief: Hands-on, interactive, participatory museum for children and
their caregivers.

Location: (Until 1999) in Paseos Mall. (New location —1999) at the Vizcaya
Metrorail Station.

Hours: Monday–Thursday, 10 A.M. to 5 P.M.; Friday, 10 A.M. to 9 P.M.; Saturday and Sunday, 11 A.M. to 6 P.M. (Mall hours are longer.)

Admissions: Under 1, free; all others, $4; senior discount available. (New
admissions charges have not been set.)

Children learn by playing at the Miami Youth Museum.

Other sites of interest nearby: Miami Museum of Science, Vizcaya and the Seaquarium (all within 5 miles), plus the many other tourist attractions in Miami.

For further information write to the Miami Youth Museum (after 1999 — Miami Children's Museum), Paseos Mall, 3301 Coral Way Level U., Miami, Florida 33145, or call (305) 446-4FUN (4386).

Museum of Discovery & Science
Ft. Lauderdale, Florida

The Museum of Discovery & Science in Ft. Lauderdale, like most children's museums, started on a small scale in a house on the river. Today, the larger new facility includes an IMAX 3D Theater along with hundreds of hands-on exhibits. Visitors can hang out with bats (and explore Florida's Everglades), be charmed by a 12-foot snake or hundreds of bees, pet a green iguana, wrap themselves in a giant bubble or become a human hurricane.

Info in brief: A hands-on science museum and IMAX 3D Theater targeting children of all age ranges and their caregivers.

Location: Downtown Ft. Lauderdale.

Hours: (Museum) Monday–Saturday, 10 A.M. to 5 P.M.; Sunday, noon to 6 P.M. (IMAX 3D Theater shows) Monday–Saturday, 10 A.M., 11:30, 12:45 P.M., 2, 3:15, 4:30, 5:45, 7, 8:15, 9:30 and 10:45 (Friday and Saturday only); Sunday, noon, 1:15, 2:30, 3:45, 5, 6:15, 7:30, and 8:45 P.M. Open everyday except Christmas.

Admissions: (Exhibits) under 3, free; children (3–12), $5; adults, $6; seniors (65+), $5. (IMAX 3D Theater) children, $9; adults, $8; seniors, $7. (Combo tickets) children, $10.50; adults, $12.50; seniors, $11.50. Member ASTC.

Unique exhibits: IMAX 3D Theater.

Other sites of interest nearby: South Florida beaches, Miami tourist attractions, and more.

For further information write to the Museum of Discovery & Science, 401 S.W. Second St., Ft. Lauderdale, Florida 33312, or call (954) 467-6637. Website: http://gsni.com/discsci.

The Orlando Science Center
Orlando, Florida

The new $44 million Orlando Science Center opened its doors in February of 1997. This huge four-story structure is filled with hands-on exhibits, interactive performance areas, science experiments, and more. Visitors can watch a large-format film, see a planetarium show or watch a laser light show at the $1.5 million Dr. Phillips CineDome. The other major area is the Darden Adventure Theater, where a performing arts company performs various full-scale theater productions throughout the day.

Visitors enter the complex through a glass skywalk from the 600-space parking deck. The main lobby that greets them is open to all four floors and houses a natural habitat with trees, birds and aquatic wildlife.

The first floor (ground floor) offers KidsTown for toddlers through elementary ages with numerous rooms designed for kids to see at their own eye-level. Exhibits include water play, a tree to climb, a bubble machine, phones, see-through fire hydrant and more.

The second floor contains NatureWorks, an exhibit of more than 100 native Floridian wildlife. Guides give continuous talks on the wildlife in the area.

The third floor contains The Cosmic Tourist, an area where visitors can discover how much their suitcases would weigh on every planet, and more.

The fourth floor contains an observatory and The BodyZone, where visitors enter through a giant mouth and step on a squishy tongue to explore how the body works. Tech Works, also on this floor, gives visitors a look at light power and how scientists and filmmakers use animation and models to find out how dinosaurs moved or what people looked like 100 years ago.

Info in brief: One of the largest and newest children's museums in the country. Plan to spend most of a day here. As this museum had just opened at the time of this writing, it is suggested that you contact the museum before visiting. Hours and admissions were subject to change.

Location: On Princeton St., off I-4 in Loch Haven Park, across from the Orange County Historical Museum, the Orlando Museum of Art and the Civic Theatres of Florida.

Hours: Monday–Thursday, 9 A.M. to 5 P.M.; Friday and Saturday, 9 A.M. to 9 P.M.; Sunday, noon to 5 P.M. CineDome open Wednesday–Saturday evenings. Cosmic concerts are shown Friday and Saturday evenings.

Admissions: (Single Adventure Passes to the exhibits) children, $6.50; adults, $8; seniors, $7. (CineDome) children, $4.50; adults, $6; seniors, $5.50. (Planetarium shows) children, $3.50; adults, $5; seniors, $4.50. (Double Adventure — any 2 of the above) children, $9.50; adults, $12; seniors, $11. (Triple Adventure — all of the above) children $11.50; adults, $14; seniors, $13. Memberships available. Member ASTC.

Other sites of interest nearby: Church Street Station sites, Disney World and the Disney World theme areas, Sea World, Wet 'n Wild, and other Orlando tourist attractions.

For further information write to The Orlando Science Center, 777 E. Princeton St., Orlando, Florida 32803, or call 1-888-OSC-4FUN or (407) 514-2114.

The School Board of Seminole County Student Museum and Center for the Social Studies
Sanford, Florida

The Student Museum is supported and operated by the Seminole County Public Schools. The emphasis is on a total approach to social studies education through hands-on experiences. The main exhibit theme areas are the Lobby (containing a photographic essay of Seminole County), the Pioneer Room, the Native American Room, a Turn of the Century Classroom, and Grandma's Attic.

The building itself was erected in 1902 and is the fourth oldest school in continuous use in Florida. It is one of the few surviving examples in Florida of Victorian school architecture at the turn of the century, and was placed on the National Register of Historic Places in 1984.

Info in brief: A hands-on children's museum with an emphasis on historic artifacts and events in Seminole County.

Hours: Open to the public — weekdays, 8 A.M. to 3:30 P.M. Closed when school groups are scheduled. Be sure to contact the museum before visiting.

Admissions: No admissions charge.

Other sites of interest nearby: Disney World, Sea World, and other Orlando tourist attractions, the Sanford Museum, the Seminole County Historical Museum, Geneva Museum, Lawton House in Oviedo, the Central Florida Zoo, and more.

For further information write to the Seminole County Public School Student Museum, 301 W. Seventh St., Sanford, Florida 32771, or call (407) 322-1902 or FAX (407) 324-4607.

South Florida Science Museum
West Palm Beach, Florida

The South Florida Science Museum is a hands-on museum for kids. At the same site, but under separate admissions fees, is the Dreher Park Zoo.

For further information write to the South Florida Science Museum, 4801 Dreher Trail North, West Palm Beach, Florida 33405, phone: (407) 832-1988. Member ASTC.

The Teddy Bear Museum of Naples
Naples, Florida

With over 3,000 teddy bears on display, this unique museum caters to a unique audience. Most children are fascinated with the display, which contains miniature to life-size, antique, limited editions and one-of-a-kind treasures.

Info in brief: Although not strictly a children's museum, a short visit to the Teddy Bear Museum would likely be memorable to any child who has ever owned a teddy bear.

Hours: Wednesday–Saturday, 10 A.M. to 5 P.M.; Sunday, 1 P.M. to 5 P.M.; Monday (December 1–April 30 only) 10 A.M. to 5 P.M.

Admissions: Adults, $6; seniors, $4; ages 4 and up, $2.

Unique exhibits: 3,000 teddy bears!

Other sites of interest nearby: Naples Princess cruises, Wooten's Everglades Adventure, Caribbean Gardens, Thomas Edison/Henry Ford Winter Estates (Ft. Myers).

For further information write to The Teddy Bear Museum of Naples, 2511 Pine Ridge Rd., Naples, Florida, or call (941) 598-2711.

Young at Art Children's Museum
Plantation, Florida

A unique art-centered hands-on museum that features an ever-changing number of educational exhibits and activities. Four permanent displays offer children (and their caregivers) opportunities to explore using a computer, a "Recycle Art Center," a "PlaySpace" which includes a "texture tunnel," a puppet theater and a LEGO construction site.

Gallery features and changing exhibits add to the variety of art experiences available. School tours, outreach programs, art classes and workshops are also offered at the museum.

Location: At the Fountains Shoppes of Distinction in Plantation, Florida.

Hours: Monday–Saturday, 11 A.M. to 5 P.M.; Sunday, noon to 5 P.M.; closed some Mondays; closed Thanksgiving and Christmas Day.

Admissions: Under 2, free; others, $3. Memberships available.

Other sites of interest nearby: Atlantic Ocean beaches, other Florida tourist attractions.

For further information write to the Young at Art Children's Museum, 801 S. University Dr., Plantation, Florida 33324, or call (954) 424-0085.

Recycle Art Center of the Young at Art Children's Museum.

Georgia

Georgia Agrirama
Tifton, Georgia

Georgia's Agrirama depicts Georgia's culture in the years between the Civil War and the early 1900s. Visitors can "experience" life through hands-on displays in this 95-acre living history museum. The "museum" is divided into five areas: a traditional farm community of the 1870s; a progressive farmstead of the 1890s; an industrial complex with water-powered grist mill, steam-powered train and sawmill; an early 1900s rural town with a drugstore containing a marble top soda fountain that sells Coca-Cola floats, a print shop, a commissary, a cotton gin and more; and The Shepherd Barn which houses the metal, fuel-powered peanut combine developed by James L. Shepherd. There are more than 35 restored structures on the site, staffed by costumed interpreters. Many of these buildings are used in the hands-on education programs.

Be sure to contact the museum before visiting, as many special events are held throughout the year.

Info in brief: A village museum or "living history museum" with items of particular interest to children. Most hands-on experiences are directed by the interpreters, and not all children will be able to enjoy such an experience, unless they are part of a group or special tour. The barnyard animals and many of the farmyard buildings are "explorable," however.

Location: I-75 Exit 20 in Tifton.

Hours: (September–May) Monday–Saturday, 9 A.M. to 5 P.M. Closed Sundays; (June–August) Tuesday–Saturday, 9 A.M. to 5 P.M.; Sunday, 12:30 P.M. to 5 P.M. Closed Mondays.

Admissions: Under 4, free; children (4–18), $4; seniors (55+), $6; adults, $8; family pass, $22. Annual passes available. Group rates available.

Other sites of interest nearby: Liberty Farms Animal Park (Valdosta); Crystal Beach & Water Park (Irwinville); Presidential Pathways region; Macon attractions such as Georgia Music Hall of Fame, Ocmulgee National Monument and "Lights on Macon" (a self-guided historic homes tour); Georgia's Stone Mountain; Six Flags Over Georgia (Atlanta), and more.

For further information write to Georgia's Agrirama, P.O. Box Q, Tifton, Georgia 31793, or call (912) 386-3344.

Hawaii

Children's Discovery Center
formerly The Hawaii Children's Museum
Honolulu, Hawaii

Founded in 1985 as a not-for-profit, community organization, the museum did not officially open its doors until 1990 at its temporary site in the Dole Cannery Square in Lwilei under the name of the Hawaii Children's Museum. The 5,000 sq. ft. hands-on museum is a successful step toward a permanent location which is projected to open in 1998. The new 37,000 sq. ft. facility will be the first of its kind to open as part of a waterfront redevelopment plan and is currently under construction. More than 200 exhibits will be available for exploration.

The new facility will use a staff of 12 full-time employees, and plans call for around 200 volunteers to work at least four hours a day. Currently, only the director and secretary are on staff.

Info in brief: Both the old and new facilities are hands-on science and humanities museums for children.

Location: (1996) the Dole Cannery Square, 650 Lwilei Road. (1998) next to the Kakaako waterfront park — in the former Kewalo incinerator facilities.

Hours: Tuesday–Friday, 9 A.M. to 1 P.M.; Saturday and Sunday, 10 A.M. to 4 P.M. Also open 10 A.M. to 4 P.M. Memorial Day (closed all other Mondays). Be sure to contact the museum for the new facility's hours.

Admissions: Children, $3; adults, $5. New facility admissions charges should be the same.

Other sites of interest nearby: The many tourist attractions in Hawaii.

For further information write to Children's Discovery Center, Ward Warehouse, Second Floor, 1050 Ala Moana Blvd., #A27, Honolulu, Hawaii 96814, or call (808) 592-KIDS (5437) or FAX (808) 592-5433.

Idaho

The Discovery Center of Idaho
Boise, Idaho

The Discovery Center of Idaho is a children's science museum with over 150 hands-on exhibits, the beginning of the scaled Solar System Walk along the greenbelt in Boise, Science Saturday classes, summer camps, demonstrations, special exhibitions and lectures, and more. A portable STARLAB is also sponsored by the Center and travels throughout the state.

The Solar System Walk begins at the Discovery Center, where the ½-meter model sun sets the scale for both the planet sizes and the distances through the entire model. Each planet appears on one of nine bronze plaques placed in various Boise parks. The museum provides visitors with a written tour guide for "visiting" the planets.

Info in brief: Large hands-on science museum for children and their caregivers.

Location: 131 Myrtle Street, between Broadway and Capitol Boulevard.

Hours: (Summer — June–August) Tuesday–Saturday, 10 A.M. to 5 P.M.; Sunday, noon to 5 P.M. (Winter — September–May) Tuesday–Friday, 9 A.M. to 5 P.M.; Saturday, 10 A.M. to 5 P.M.; Sunday, noon to 5 P.M. Closed Mondays, Thanksgiving, Christmas and New Year's Day.

Admissions: Under 3, free; children (3–18), $2.50; adults, $4; seniors (60+), $3. Memberships available. Member ASTC.

Unique exhibits: Solar System Model Walk (see information above).

Other sites of interest nearby: Boise Zoo, MK Nature Center, Old Idaho Penitentiary, Boise Art Museum, World Center for Birds of Prey, Museum of Mining & Geology, Idaho Museum of Military History, Idaho Botanical Garden, The Basque Museum, and the Idaho Historical Museum.

For further information write to The Discovery Center of Idaho, P.O. Box 192, Boise, Idaho 83701, or call (208) 343-9895 or FAX (208) 343-0105.

Illinois

The Art Institute of Chicago
Chicago, Illinois

Although The Art Institute of Chicago is not a normal hands-on museum for children, a new interactive exhibition will offer hands-on opportunities for children until sometime in 1999. The new space in the Kraft Education center (which normally caters to children and their families) has been designed by award-winning Chicago architect Stanley Tigerman and features six Masterworks from the Art Institute's own collection. Each object tells a story and is installed in its own dynamic setting. Hands-on space for children, ages 7 to 12, is provided with computers, writing tables, a puppet stage, and games which will encourage children to explore these carefully-chosen objects from around the world.

Stanley Tigerman looks at an installation model with one of the children who helped design the Masterworks setting (PHOTOGRAPH BY AVIS MANDEL).

The six works of art are Bernardo Martorell's painting, "St. George Killing the Dragon" (1430/35); the 16th-century bronze "Statue of a Standing Vishnu"; John Quidor's painting, "Rip Van Winkle" (1829); the 19th-century "Nigerian Royal Altar Tusk"; Walter Ellison's painting, "Train Station" (1936); and Martina Lopez's digital photograph, "Heirs Come to Pass" (1991).

Info in brief: An art museum/institute which will offer special hands-on art experiences for children until the new millennium. Other special children's activities are also offered year-round at the Kraft Education center.

Hours: Monday, Wednesday, Thursday and Friday, 10:30 A.M. to 4:30 P.M.; Tuesday, 10:30 A.M. to 8 P.M.; Saturday, 10 A.M. to 5 P.M.; Sunday and holidays, noon to 5 P.M.

Admissions: Children, $3.50; students, $3.50; adults, $7; seniors, $3.50. Tuesdays are free admissions days. Closed Thanksgiving and Christmas Day. Memberships available.

For further information write to The Art Institute of Chicago, 111 S. Michigan Ave., Chicago, Illinois 60603-6110, or call (312) 443-3600 (TDD 443-3890).

Chicago Children's Museum
Chicago, Illinois

Exhibits at the Chicago Children's Museum focus on newsgathering or medical technology (hospital exhibit).

For further information write to the Chicago Children's Museum, 435 E. Illinois St., Chicago, Illinois 60611. Member ASTC.

Discovery Center Museum
Rockford, Illinois

The Discovery Center is a participatory museum designed to provide hands-on learning experiences for visitors of all ages. The targeted audience is preschool through junior high ages, and the caregivers are encouraged to participate with their children.

Founded in 1980, the museum moved into its current 26,000 sq. ft. facility in 1991, where it shares the Riverfront Museum Park building with five other cultural organizations. The museum was visited by Elizabeth Dole in 1996.

Permanent exhibits explore the areas of sound (a walk-on piano is featured here), newscasting (a state-of-the-art news studio is here), and art

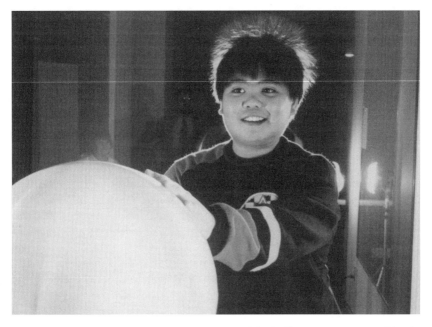

A visitor to the Discovery Center Museum in Rockford, Illinois, is entertained by the electrostatic generator.

(one gallery is devoted to color and light experimentation and includes a video art exhibit, prisms, bubbles and more). Other permanent exhibits include "Body Shop," where families can learn about bodies and how they function, nutrition, genetics, fingerprinting and agility. In "Tot Spot," preschoolers are offered role-playing and tactile experiences. The "Space" exhibit includes a planetarium, space photographs, a gravity well, Geochron clock, a Bernoulli blower and a collection of NASA photos. Rock River Discovery Park is an outdoor play and exploration area offering a cave, locks and dams, Newton's cradle, automated kinetic ball towers, pendulum swings and whisper dishes. In May of 1992, it was listed by CHILD magazine as one of the ten best outdoor facilities of its kind in the nation.

Info in brief: A sophisticated hands-on museum and outdoor play and exploration area especially for children.

Location: In Riverfront Museum Park, a cultural center along the Rock River in downtown Rockford, approximately 90 minutes northwest of Chicago off I-90.

Hours: (Winter) Tuesday–Saturday, 11 A.M. to 5 P.M.; Sunday, noon to 5 P.M.; open Mondays on school holidays. (Summer) Monday–Saturday, 10 A.M. to 5 P.M.; Sunday, noon to 5 P.M.

Admissions: Under 2, free; children, $2.50; adults, $3; seniors, $2.50. Memberships available. Member ASTC.

For further information write to Discovery Center Museum, 711 N. Main St., Rockford, Illinois 61103, or call (815) 963-6769 or FAX (815) 968-0164. E-mail: med@discntr.com.

Kohl Children's Museum
Wilmette, Illinois

The Kohl Children's Museum opened in 1985, building on the success of its predecessor, the Kohl Teacher Center, a pioneer Chicago resource since 1973. The museum encourages hands-on learning as one of the most effective modes of learning, and caters to children ages 1 to 8 years of age. Imaginative play is greatly emphasized.

Besides the museum proper and its exhibits, Kohl offers field trips, focused programs, summer camps, workshops, seminars, special events, after-school programs, free daily art, cultural and science activities, and more.

Current exhibits include "Construction," "H_2O," "Long Ago and Far Away," "People," "Jewel/Osco," "Chagall for Children," "All Aboard" (CTA train), "Recycle Arts," and "Duplo Room."

Info in brief: Hands-on, interactive, imaginative experiences for children ages 1 to 8.

Hours: Tuesday–Saturday, 9 A.M. to 5 P.M.; Sunday, noon to 5 P.M.

Admissions: Under 1, free; seniors, $3; adults and children, $4. Memberships available.

Other sites of interest nearby: The many Chicago tourist attractions.

For further information write to Kohl Children's Museum, 165 Green Bay Road, Wilmette, Illinois 60091, or call (847) 256-6056.

The Science Center
Carbondale, Illinois

For further information contact: The Science Center, P.O. Box 4041, 611 E. College, Carbondale, Illinois 62901, phone: (618) 529-5431. Member ASTC.

SciTech
Science and Technology Interactive Center
Aurora, Illinois

In 1989, a 7,000 sq. ft. building in Naperville was donated for the temporary housing of a science museum. By the following year, SciTech signed a 10-year lease with the City of Aurora for the use of its former post office in downtown Aurora (listed on the historic register). The museum now hosts more than 200 exhibits on physics, chemistry and mathematics, going from a strictly volunteer-run organization to a 44-employee-plus-volunteers museum.

Sci-Tech's mission is to "provide a cultural resource focusing on science and technology for a broad general audience." One aspect of this mission is to encourage children to participate in many of the exhibits. This is done through activities at the museum and in the community.

In the community, SciTech offers "Museum in a School," traveling chemistry demonstrations and the "Hook 'Em While They're Young" program. Museum programs include the "Student Explainer Program," "Discover & Explore," SciTech clubs for girls, field trips and focused field trips, science camps and classes, along with more than 200 permanent exhibits. Three science activity rooms, an auditorium and a solar telescope are also in-house.

Info in brief: Strictly a science museum with a broad range of hands-on activities for children.

Location: In the historic district on Stolp Island in downtown Aurora, in the old Post Office building.

Hours: Wednesday, Friday and Sunday, noon to 5 P.M.; Thursday, noon to 8 P.M. (no charge after 5 P.M.); Saturday, 10 A.M. to 5 P.M.

Admissions: Adults (over 18), $4; seniors, $2; children over 2 and students, $2; family, $8. Member of the Association of Youth Museums. Member ASTC.

Unique exhibitions: Large number of science participatory experiment-type exhibits.

Other sites of interest nearby: Fermi National Accelerator Laboratory, Illinois Mathematics and Science Academy, Blackberry Farm, and Red Oak Nature Center.

For further information write to SciTech, 18 W. Benton, Aurora, Illinois 60506, or call (630) 859-3434 or FAX (630) 859-8692. Web site: http://town.hall.org/places/SciTech.

Spertus Museum
Spertus Institute of Jewish Studies
Chicago, Illinois

The mission of the Spertus Museum is to "preserve and disseminate the intellectual, cultural, social and spiritual legacy of the Jewish past and demonstrate its continuing relevance to the present." Established in 1968, it includes seven galleries and approximately 12,000 sq. ft. of exhibition space.

Permanent exhibits include the Zell Holocaust Memorial, Rosebaum ARTiFACT Center for children, and the Gallery of the Generations, along with rotating exhibits throughout the year. Family programs, after-school programs and school programs are also offered.

Info in brief: The museum is basically an historical and art museum with items specifically for children, but of interest to all ages.

Location: 618 S. Michigan Ave., Chicago.

Hours: Sunday–Thursday, 10 A.M. to 5 P.M.; Friday, 10 A.M. to 3 P.M.; closed Saturday.

Admissions: Adults, $4; children, students and seniors, $2.

Unique exhibits: Most comprehensive Judaic collection in the Midwest.

Other sites of interest nearby: Many Chicago tourist attractions.

For further information write to the Spertus Museum, 618 S. Michigan Avenue, Chicago, Illinois 60605, or call (312) 922-9012 or FAX (312) 922-6406. E-mail: sijs@spertus.edu.

Indiana

The Children's Museum of Indianapolis
Indianapolis, Indiana

As of January 1, 1997, the Indianapolis Children's Museum was the largest children's museum in the world. From its beginnings in a small carriage house in 1925, the museum aimed to encourage children to enrich their lives through learning and exploring. The current 356,000 sq. ft. museum now houses ten major galleries which offer exhibits in the physical and natural sciences, history, foreign cultures and the arts, continuing the original mission.

The Children's Museum of Indianapolis.

The present site offers an IWERKS CineDome Theater, an Outdoor Festival Park and Clowes Garden Gallery, a Welcome Center, and hundreds of hands-on permanent and changing exhibits. The galleries are connected by a sky-lit open core, with zig-zagging ramps rising 70 feet to the top level. Some of the exhibits on permanent display include a Victorian railway depot, "Space-Quest Planetarium," "What If...," "Mysteries in History" (which includes an authentic 1830s cabin and a 1900s downtown street on the fourth level of the museum), and the Eli Lilly Center for Exploration, to name a few. The Eli Lilly Center is the museum's largest gallery with 15,000 sq. ft. of exhibits and explorations especially for children ages 10 to 18. On the fifth level is an actual working carousel (50¢ charge) along with other toys and play activities.

Besides the more than 110,000 artifacts at the museum, special outreach programs, workshops and events are also sponsored by the museum. More than 180 full-time and 200 part-time staff members, along with more than 850 volunteers, help to keep the museum running smoothly.

Location: On 13 acres of land in Indianapolis' central city.

Hours: (Labor Day–February) Tuesday–Sunday, 10 A.M. to 5 P.M.; (March–August) open daily, 10 A.M. to 5 P.M.; first Thursday of each month, 5 P.M. to 8 P.M., free of charge. Free admissions on Martin Luther King and Presidents' days. Closed Thanksgiving and Christmas Day.

Admissions: (Museum only) under 2, free; children (2–17), $3; adults, $6; seniors, $5. (CineDome) under 2, free; children (2–17), $4.50; adults, $6.50; seniors, $6.50. After 6 P.M., all seats are $6.50. (Planetarium) $2. (Lilly Theater) Summer, all seats $2; Fall, all seats $3. Some combined tickets are available at slightly lower prices. Memberships are available. Member of ASTC and AYM.

Unique characteristic: Largest children's museum in the world; working carousel on the fifth level.

For further information write to The Children's Museum, 3000 N. Meridian St., Indianapolis, Indiana 46208-4716, or call 1-800-208KIDS or (317) 924-5431. Website: http://www.al.com/children/home.html.

Children's Science & Technology Museum
Terre Haute, Indiana

For further information contact: Children's Science & Technology Museum, 523 Wabash Ave., Terre Haute, Indiana 47802, phone: (812) 235-5548. Member ASTC.

College Football Hall of Fame
South Bend, Indiana

The College Football Hall of Fame opened in South Bend, Indiana, in August of 1995 and advertises itself as one of the most interactive sports museums in the nation. The Hall offers an innovative 360-degree "Stadium Theater" which surrounds the viewer with the sights and sounds of a college game. Other exhibits include the "Hall of Champions," with memorabilia and artifacts; "Pigskin Pageantry," where the traditions that accompany the game are celebrated; "The Training Center," where visitors can test their football skills through a series of interactive, fun-filled challenges and activities; and "Record Breakers," containing artifacts from record-breaking games. Also at the museum is a 43-foot-high sculpture—"Pursuit of a Dream," a football resource library, the Gridiron Plaza (19,000 sq. ft. area) in front of the museum (available for rent), and the Press Box (4,300 sq. ft. also available for rent).

Info in brief: A collections museum with lots of interactive exhibits and a few actual hands-on activities for kids.

Location: Downtown South Bend.

Hours: Daily, 9 A.M. to 7 P.M. Closed Christmas, New Year's and Thanksgiving Day.

College Football Hall of Fame in South Bend, Indiana.

Admissions: 5 and under, free; children (6–14), $4; adults, $9; adults (St. Joseph County residents), $7; seniors, $6.

Unique exhibits: Largest collection of historic college football artifacts anywhere in the world; also, possibly the most interactive sports museum in the United States.

Other sites of interest nearby: The Northern Indiana Center for History.

For further information write to the College Football Hall of Fame, 111 S. St. Joseph St., South Bend, Indiana 46601, or call 1-800-440-FAME (3263) or (219) 235-9999 or FAX (219) 235-5720. Website: http://collegefootball.org/

kidsfirst Children's Museum
South Bend, Indiana

The Northern Indiana Center for History is located on a ten-acre site in the historic West Washington District in South Bend. The site includes the Copshaholm House, the Center for History, the Worker's Home Museum, and kidsfirst Children's Museum. kidsfirst Children's Museum is an interactive history museum where children can experience a farmer's field as it might appear to an earthworm, participate in a demonstration of the basic food groups, work in an archaeology dig, sit in a wigwam or canoe, run a printing press or computer, and more. The other museums offer a variety of exhibits and collections mainly focusing on the St. Joseph River Valley history and geology. For further information on each of these museums, write to the Center.

Info in brief: kidsfirst is a hands-on museum for children and their caregivers.

Location: West Washington Historic District in downtown South Bend.

Hours: Tuesday–Saturday, 10 A.M. to 5 P.M.; Sunday, noon to 5 P.M.

Admissions: Small admissions charge for each museum — contact the Center for exact details.

For further information write to kidsfirst Children's Museum, Northern Indiana Center for History, 808 W. Washington, South Bend, Indiana 46601, or call (219) 235-9664 or FAX (219) 235-9059.

Muncie Children's Museum
Muncie, Indiana

The Muncie Children's Museum, originally opened in the early 1970s, opened a new facility in July 1996. The new facility has 24,000 sq. ft. of exhibit space and employs about 15 people on staff.

A wide variety of exhibits are available, including: "Digging into the Past" (paleontology); "Don't Be a Drip, Go with the Flow" (water activities); "Guts and Stuff" (a Stuffee soft sculptured doll featuring removable internal organs); "Learn Not to Burn"; "Under Indiana" (the geology of Indiana); "Middletown" (variety of changeable storefronts for role-playing); "Garfield Theater" (allows children to interact with Garfield in a cartoon using blue screen technology); and more. An outdoor learning center, a computer lab, a reading loft, a giant locomotive, an actual semi-tractor, and a model train layout are also available for the visitor's use.

Info in brief: A hands-on, participatory museum for children and their caregivers.

Hours: Tuesday–Saturday, 10 A.M. to 5 P.M.; Sunday, 1 P.M. to 5 P.M.

Admissions: $4.

Unique exhibits: As Jim Davis, Garfield's creator, lives in Muncie; he has been instrumental in establishing the Garfield exhibit — the only one of its kind in the nation.

For further information write to the Muncie Children's Museum, 515 S. High St., Muncie, Indiana 47305, or call (317) 286-1660.

Science Central
Fort Wayne, Indiana

Science Central is a hands-on science museum for school-aged children and their caregivers. All exhibits focus on the skills that scientists use: measurement, observation, prediction, classification and inference. Visitors are encouraged to ask questions and participate in all activities and experiments. Exhibits offer instruction about weather, the ocean, earth forces, and more. The main changing exhibits gallery offers new exhibits approximately four times a year.

Info in brief: A hands-on science museum offering the "real stuff" of science to be explored, offering sophisticated equipment and technology.

Location: Downtown Fort Wayne.

Hours & Admissions: New brochures were being planned at the time of this publication. Be sure to contact the museum for updated information. Member ASTC.

Other sites of interest nearby: Historic Fort Wayne, Fun Spot Amusement Park in Angola, Indiana Beach in Monticello.

For further information write to Science Central, 1950 N. Clinton St., Fort Wayne, Indiana 46805-4049, or call (219) 424-2400 or 1-800-4HANDS-ON or FAX (219) 422-2899.

Iowa

Family Museum of Arts and Science
Bettendorf, Iowa

A proposal written in 1990 by a manager of arts programming for the City of Bettendorf called for a complex near the center of the community where residents could have access to library facilities, art and dance classes, a hands-on museum, and more in the proposed "center for learning," now retitled "The Learning Campus." In a few short years, the museum opened (1997) and now offers five main in-house hands-on exhibits in its 9,600 sq.

ft. of gallery space, as well as outreach programs in science, and the visual and performing arts. More exhibits are already in the process of being built.

The five interactive exhibits currently on display are "The Homestead" (touch a 10-foot-tall tornado, create a lightning bolt, control soil erosion, climb a tree house, etc.); "Kinder Garten" (a pre-schoolers area which celebrates the strong German heritage of the area); "Heartland" (Heartbeat Cafe, Cardiac Cruiser, Hemobile, and more); "Rhythm Alley" (activities with sound, music and a psychedelic shadowbox encourage visitors to explore and create); "Brainstorms" (examples of the inventive genius of dreamers and doers).

Info in brief: A hands-on museum with activities for pre-schoolers through middle-schoolers and their families.

Location: On Learning Campus Drive in the 2900 Block of 18th St., next to Bettendorf Public Library and Information Center.

Hours: Monday–Thursday, 9 A.M. to 8 P.M. (exhibit gallery opens at noon on Monday); Friday and Saturday, 9 A.M. to 5 P.M.; Sunday, noon to 5 P.M.

Admissions: Under 2, free; visitors (2–59), $3; seniors (60+), $2. Member ASTC.

For further information write to the Family Museum of Arts and Science, 2900 Learning Campus Drive, Bettendorf, Iowa 52722, or call (319) 344-4106 or FAX (319) 344-4164.

Fascination Station
Ottumwa, Iowa

The idea for Fascination Station began in 1987. Doors opened on a children's museum called "The Exploratorium of Iowa" in 1988. That museum was located in an unused school building. Finally, in June of 1995, the museum moved to a more easily accessible building in downtown Ottumwa. At that time the name was changed to Fascination Station.

One full-time employee oversees several volunteers who help to keep the more than 50 hands-on exhibits up and running. Exhibits include laser art activities, a bicycle generator, a moon walk and hovercraft area, tactile tunnel, "Robot Arm," skeleton and human torso, "Plasmasphere," a black light room, a bubblemaker, mind puzzles, a catenary arch, optical illusions and more. Special events and classes are also scheduled regularly throughout the year.

Info in brief: A small hands-on children's museum.

Location: Downtown Ottumwa between Main and Second streets.

Hours: Sunday–Friday, 1 P.M. to 5 P.M.; Saturday, 10 A.M. to 5 P.M. Summer hours are longer (contact museum before visiting).

Admissions: Under 3, free; all others, $2.50.

Other sites of interest nearby: The Wapello County Historical Society, The Beach Ottumwa water park, The American Gothic House in Eldon, the Antique Air Power Museum near Blakesburg, and the Wilderness Kingdom Zoo near Floris.

For further information write to Fascination Station, 104 S. Market St., Ottumwa, Iowa 52501, or call (515) 682-0921.

The Imaginarium
Grout Museum of History and Science
Rensselaer Russell House Museum
Waterloo, Iowa

The Grout Museum has grown into a facility with three unique and separate properties — The Grout Museum of History and Science, the Rensselaer Russell House Museum and the Carl and Peggy Bluedorn Science Imaginarium.

The Grout Museum emphasizes the cultural and natural history of the region. It features permanent and changing exhibits, daily planetarium shows and the interactive "Discovery Zone" with hands-on activities for children.

The Rensselaer Russell House is one of the oldest dwellings in Black Hawk County, having been built in 1861. The house is listed on the National Register of Historic Places. Tours are offered to the public all year round.

The Imaginarium is strictly a hands-on science museum with dozens of exhibits for children. Visitors can grab the controls of the laser spirograph and create a laser show; participate in a bubble race, shoot a ring of air across the room with an air cannon, ride a life-size gyroscope, spin on a turntable platform, and more. Live science demonstrations and experiments are also offered daily.

Info in brief: Three separate museums, two of which offer hands-on experiences for children. The Imaginarium is a strictly hands-on museum for children and their caregivers. The Grout Museum has one area, "The Discovery Zone," with hands-on experiences for young children.

Location: The Grout Museum District — off South Street in Waterloo. Grout Museum, 503 South St.; Rensselaer Russell House Museum, 520 W. 3rd St.; Imaginarium, 322 Washington St.

Hours: Grout Museum and Imaginarium — (June–August) Tuesday–Saturday, 10 A.M. to 4:30 P.M.; (September–May) Tuesday–Friday, 1 P.M. to 4:30 P.M.; Saturday, 10 A.M. to 4:30 P.M. Imaginarium also open Sunday, 1 P.M. to 4:30 P.M. Russell House Museum — (April–May and September and October) Tuesday–Saturday, 1 P.M. to 4:30 P.M. (September and October) Tuesday–Friday, 10 A.M. to 4:30 P.M.; Saturday, 1 P.M. to 4:30 P.M.

Admissions: Under 3, free to all museums. Museum District Pass (includes 3 museums) — children, $4; adults, $6. Museum District Pass (includes 2 museums) — all visitors, $4. General admission at both the Grout and Imaginarium, $2.50. Russell House admissions — child, $1; adult, $2.50. Memberships available. Member ASTC.

Other sites of interest nearby: Cedar Rapids attractions.

For further information write to The Grout Museum of History & Science, 503 South St., Waterloo, Iowa 50701. You may also call Grout Museum, (319) 234-6357; Russell House, (319) 233-0262; or Imaginarium, (319) 233-8708.

Science Station
Cedar Rapids, Iowa

Science Station celebrated its 10th anniversary in 1995. In 1985, the historic brick fire station, built in 1917, was vacated, and the Junior League of Cedar Rapids, Inc., turned the building into a hands-on science museum. Three years later, the League turned it over to the community.

Many of the original exhibits replicated those displayed at the Exploratorium in San Francisco and other similar museums around the country, and are still being displayed, but many new displays have also been added. Microsoft Company recently sponsored a Gateway 2000 computer for running an interactive flight simulator CD on a newly built Space Control Central wall. Two other computers offer other interactive adventures.

In all, three floors of hands-on galleries, including a hologram exhibit on the second floor, are displayed. Exhibits cover areas such as Bubbles, Space & Flight, Broadcast Meteorology, Music & Sound, Light & Illusions, Nutrition, and more. Traveling exhibits are also put on display occasionally throughout the year, and special weekend programs are offered.

Info in brief: A hands-on museum for children and their caregivers.

Location: An historic, 1917 brick fire station in downtown Cedar Rapids, across from the public library.

Hours: Tuesday–Saturday, 9 A.M. to 4 P.M.; Sunday, 1 P.M. to 4 P.M. Closed Mondays and major holidays.

Admissions: Under 3, free; children (3–18), $2.50; adults (19–62), $3.50; seniors, $3. Member ASTC.

For further information write to Science Station, 427 First St., S.E., Cedar Rapids, Iowa 52401-1808, or call (319) 366-0968. Website: www.netins.net/showcase/scistation.

Kansas

The Children's Museum of Kansas City
Kansas City, Kansas

Incorporated in 1984, The Children's Museum of Kansas City moved into its permanent location in 1990. The museum is committed to reaching children of all backgrounds. Its mission is to provide "interactive, educational and entertaining exhibits and programming in a professional manner, aiming to unfold a learning journey that stimulates imagination and creative thinking."

The more than 40 hands-on exhibits are built around the themes of machinery, light, energy, science exploration and art. The targeted age range is children from 4 to 12 and their families. Touching and exploring are encouraged.

The museum also provides educational experiences in the community. Museum "teachers" visit classrooms, take field trips, and offer workshops to various groups through outreach programs such as "The Magic School Bus," youth afterschool programs and "Hands On Science Outreach" programs.

Info in brief: Hands-on, interactive, directed and nondirected activities for children and their caregivers.

Location: Lower level of Indian Springs Marketplace in Kansas City.

Hours: Tuesday–Saturday, 9:30 A.M. to 5 P.M.; Sunday, 1 P.M. to 5 P.M.; closed Monday.

Admissions: Under age 2, free; all others, $2.50. Memberships available.

Other sites of interest nearby: Kansas City Museum, Nelson-Atkins Museum of Art, Kansas City Zoo, Leavenworth County Historical Museum, Wyandotte County Museum, Worlds of Fun and more.

For further information write to The Children's Museum of Kansas City, 4601 State Ave., Kansas City, Kansas 66102, or call (913) 287-8888.

Children's Museum of Wichita
Wichita, Kansas

This children's museum is a totally hands-on facility. Exhibits and displays include a three-story (child-size "stories") maze, a gigantic puzzle of the United States, a costumes area with various careers represented, a Prairie House, a teepee, miniature antique car and airplane, and more. It is a component of the Science Center, Inc.

Info in brief: Hands-on museum especially for children.

Location: One block south of Century II in downtown Wichita.

Hours: Tuesday–Saturday, 9 A.M. to 5 P.M.; Sunday, 1 P.M. to 5 P.M.; summer hours — Monday and longer Sunday hours.

Admissions: Under 2, free; other visitors, $3. Memberships available.

Other sites of interest nearby: Omnisphere and Science Center, Sedgwick County Zoo, Wichita Boathouse & Arkansas River Foundation, Wichita Greyhound Park, Wichita International Raceway, Wichita Thunder Hockey, Wichita Wings, and more.

For further information write to the Children's Museum of Wichita, 435 S. Water, Wichita, Kansas 67202, or call (316) 267-2281, (316) 267-3844 or (316) 263-3373.

Kansas Cosmosphere & Space Center
Hutchinson, Kansas

Although the Kansas Cosmosphere & Space Center is not normally a hands-on museum during the winter, special 5-day-long camps called "Future Astronaut Training Programs" are offered for children during the summer. Participants train on sophisticated space simulators, build and launch model rockets, learn flight techniques and experience other activities which teach them what it's like to be an astronaut or work in the space program.

Discovery Workshops are also offered throughout the year. These programs are specifically developed for school-aged children, from kindergarten through 12th grade. Contact Cosmosphere before visiting for an up-to-date schedule.

Also located at the Space Center are an Omnimax Theater, Hall of Space Museum (with exhibits of space memorabilia and daily live shows demonstrating rocket power), and a new multimedia Planetarium.

Info in brief: A Space Center, Planetarium and summer camp location.

Hours: Monday–Friday, 9 A.M. to 9 P.M.; Saturday, 10 A.M. to 9 P.M.; Sunday, noon to 9 P.M. Open every day except Christmas. Contact the Space Center for Planetarium and Omnimax Theater showtimes.

Admissions: Hall of Space Museum —$2; Planetarium —$2.50; Laser Light Show —$4; Omnimax Theater — Children (12 and under), $4.75; adults, $5.50; seniors, $4.75.

Unique exhibits: The Hall of Space Museum contains the world's largest and most comprehensive collection of space suits.

Other sites of interest nearby: Kaleidoscope (Kansas City), Toy and Miniature Museum (Kansas City), Jesse James historic sites, Kansas City Zoo, NCAA Hall of Champions, American Royal Museum & Visitors Center and other Kansas City attractions.

For further information write to Kansas Cosmosphere & Space Center, 11th & Plum, Hutchinson, Kansas, or call 1-800-397-0330 or (316) 662-2305.

McPherson Museum
McPherson, Kansas

Although not a hands-on museum, the McPherson Museum offers children an opportunity to learn about things of special interest to the young. Located in the historic three-story 1920s Vaniman house, the museum is packed with historic and scientific artifacts in a relaxed, friendly atmosphere. Some of the artifacts on display and of special interest to children include a huge collection of stuffed birds and animals, an equally large collection of fossils and dinosaur artifacts, the original M-G-M lion's skin (first seen live on the M-G-M movie screen in July 1928), the first synthetic diamond, and much more. Several special events are hosted by the museum throughout the year, including the Old Fashioned Fall Harvest Festival in September which features more than 50 demonstrations of old time crafts (children can participate in some of these crafts).

Info in brief: A collections-based museum with many artifacts of special interest to children, and others of special interest to adults.

Hours: Tuesday–Sunday, 1 P.M. to 5 P.M. Closed Mondays and holidays. Tours are available upon request.

Admissions: Free (donations accepted).

Unique exhibit: Many unique artifacts on display such as the M-G-M lion skin.

Other sites of interest nearby: Historic City of Lindsborg (its strong Swedish influence draws tourists from around the world), the Maxwell Game Preserve (buffalo habitat tours available), the Mennonite museum in Gossell and the Mennonite museum in Newton.

For further information write to the McPherson Museum, 1130 E. Euclid St., McPherson, Kansas 67460, or call (316) 245-2574.

The Omnisphere & Science Center
Wichita, Kansas

The Omnisphere & Science Center is both a hands-on children's science museum and a planetarium. Live science shows are also offered, with scheduled shows changing seasonally. A model railroad is on display Saturdays only.

In the Science Center are approximately 80 hands-on science exhibits, including the anti-gravity mirror, the harmonograph (which makes spirographical designs), a VanDeGraaff Generator, and plenty of telescopes and microscopes to allow visitors to study the stars, crystal structures, tiny insects, and other microscopic life.

Info in brief: A hands-on children's museum which also offers live demonstrations, planetarium shows and a model railroad display.

Location: Downtown Wichita.

Hours: Science Center — Tuesday–Friday, 8 A.M. to 5 P.M.; Saturday and Sunday, 1 P.M. to 5 P.M. Model railroad open on Saturday only. Planetarium and science shows schedules vary, usually at 1 P.M., 2 P.M. and 3 P.M., but be sure to contact the museum before visiting for exact scheduling details.

Admissions: $2 museum admission plus $1 per show.

Other sites of interest nearby: Sedgewick County Zoo, Sportsworld, Wichita Greyhound Park, Wichita International Raceway, Wichita Thunder Hockey, Wichita Wings, Wichita Wranglers, Wichita Center for the Arts, Wichita Children's Theatre and Dance Center, Children's Museum of Wichita (see listing) and more.

For further information write to Omnisphere & Science Center, 220 S. Main, Wichita, Kansas 67202, or call (316) 337-9174.

Louisville Science Center
Louisville, Kentucky

Founded in 1871 as a part of the Public Library System of Kentucky, the Louisville Science Center is one of the oldest children's museums in the country. Following a few name and location changes, the museum is now located

Louisville Science Center.

in five restored 19th-century cast-iron warehouse buildings on Louisville's historic Main Street, and has become Kentucky's largest hands-on science center. Three floors of permanent and temporary exhibits are on display, teaching visitors about science and natural history topics. An IMAX Theater, a Space Science Gallery with space missions artifacts, a mummy's tomb (including a 3,400-year-old mummy), and "A Show of Hands" (a multi-disciplinary exhibit that explores the human hand) are also on display. Interactive science demonstrations and mini-plays are presented daily.

The Center adopted a new mission statement along with its new name in 1994. Visitors can expect to see several changes and improvements to the site over the next few years.

Info in brief: A hands-on and interactive science and natural history museum for children and all members of the family.

Location: Downtown Louisville's historic Main Street, in five restored 19th-century cast-iron warehouse buildings.

Hours: Monday–Thursday, 10 A.M. to 5 P.M.; Friday and Saturday, 10 A.M. to 9 P.M.; Sunday, noon to 5 P.M.

Admissions: (Science Center only) children (2–12), $4.25; adults, $5.25; seniors (60+), $4.25. (Science Center & IMAX Theater) children (2–12), $5.50; adults, $7; seniors (60+), $5.50. Memberships available. Member ASTC.

Other sites of interest nearby: Louisville Slugger Museum, Kentucky Derby Museum, Kentucky Kingdom amusement park, Louisville Zoo, and Fall of the Ohio Interpretive Center.

For further information write to the Louisville Science Center, 727 W. Main St., Louisville, Kentucky, 40202-2681, or call (502) 561-6103 or FAX (502) 561-6145.

Louisville Science Center
Louisville, Kentucky

For further information contact: Louisville Science Center, 727 W. Main St., Louisville, Kentucky 40202, phone: (502) 561-6103. Member ASTC.

Louisiana

The Children's Museum of Lake Charles
Lake Charles, Louisiana

Incorporated in 1988, the Children's Museum of Lake Charles was housed in an unused school building. In 1991, it relocated to its current location near the Charpentier Historic District. Hundreds of volunteers help the two full-time and three part-time staff in maintaining the facility, setting up exhibits and staffing special events.

Exhibits encourage visitors to explore the social sciences, science and technology, and the visual and performing arts. Although the targeted age range is 3 to 14 years of age, the hands-on, participatory exhibits are of interest to all ages.

Info in brief: A hands-on exploratory museum for children of all ages and their caregivers.

Location: Near the Charpentier Historic District in Lake Charles.

Hours: Tuesday–Saturday, 10 A.M. to 5 P.M. (Other hours are for tours only.)

Admissions: Small admissions fee.

For further information write to The Children's Museum of Lake Charles, 925 Enterprise Blvd., Lake Charles, Louisiana 70601.

Louisiana Children's Museum
New Orleans, Louisiana

At the Louisiana Children's Museum, explorations in math, science and physics have been the main focus since 1986. Originally situated in 8,000 sq. ft. of a 134-year-old building in New Orleans' historic warehouse district, the museum has continued to add square footage to its area, until finally purchasing the entire building in 1992. More than 45,000 sq. ft. of exhibit space now offer hundreds of activities for children from preschool age through middle school. Current exhibits include: "The Lab," math and physics experiments; "Challenges," living with disabilities; "The Times-Picayune Theatre"; "Body Works," physical fitness activities; "Kids' Cafe," pretend restaurant; "Water Works"; "Art Trek," an arts and crafts center; a working TV studio, supermarket, and more. In addition to the permanent exhibits, the museum hosts special scheduled programs, toddler activities, live performances and demonstrations, safety workshops and art workshops throughout the year.

Info in brief: A hands-on science museum for children. Now counted in the top 10 percent of children's museums according to square footage and attendance.

Location: In the historic warehouse district, between Magazine and Tchoupitoulas streets and just four blocks from the Ernest N. Morial Convention Center and other riverfront attractions.

Hours: Tuesday–Saturday, 9:30 A.M. to 4:30 P.M.; Sunday, noon to 4:30 P.M.; Monday (summer only), 9:30 A.M. to 4:30 P.M.

Admissions: $5 for all visitors over 1 year old.

Other sites of interest nearby: The many tourist attractions in New Orleans.

For further information write to the Louisiana Children's Museum, 420 Julia St., New Orleans, Louisiana 70130, or call (504) 523-1357 or FAX (504) 529-3666.

SciPort Discovery Center
Shreveport, Louisiana

In 1986, the Exploratorium opened as a children's hands-on science and humanities museum. Many changes and innovations have been undertaken, including a name change in 1993 to "SciPort." Current plans call for the Grand Opening of a larger SciPort Discovery Center facility in June of 1998. The new $15 million 67,000 sq. ft. children's museum will offer more than 200 hands-on exhibits in halls themed as the Red River Gallery, Body Works, Physical Science, Technology, Children's Discovery, and the Traveling Exhibit Hall. An IMAX Dome Theater will also be housed at this facility.

Info in brief: A hands-on science and humanities museum for children and their caregivers.

Location: (1996) 528 Commerce St. (new location, 1998) at the corner of Clyde Fant and Lake streets.

Hours: (1996) Monday–Friday, 9 A.M. to 5 P.M.; Saturday, 10 A.M. to 5 P.M.; Sunday, 1 P.M. to 5 P.M. Be sure to check with the museum for hours at the new facility.

Admissions: (1996) Under 3, free; children (3–17), $2; adults, $3; seniors, $2.50. Memberships available. Member ASTC. Be sure to check with the museum for admissions charges at the new facility.

Other sites of interest nearby: Spring Street Museum, ARK-LA Antique & Classic Vehicle Museum, R.S. Barnwell Garden & Art Center, Sports Museum of Champions, and "Spirit of the Red" River Cruises.

For further information write to the SciPort Discovery Center, (mailing address) 101 Milam St., Suite 12, Shreveport, Louisiana 71101, or call (318) 424-3466.

Maine

The Children's Museum of Maine
Portland, Maine

Celebrating its 20th anniversary in 1997, The Children's Museum of Maine offers many hands-on exhibits for children of all ages, including farming, fishing, a fire engine, banking, shopping, a computer lab, a space shuttle experience, Camera Obscura and more. At least one major theme exhibit is offered each year, with special activities, events, workshops and speakers made available for visitors at various times throughout the exhibition period, along with the permanent displays. A calendar of events is available from the museum.

Info in brief: A hands-on participatory museum for children and their caregivers with new exhibits being offered on a regular basis.

Location: Downtown Portland, 142 Free Street.

Hours: (Memorial Day to Labor Day and school vacation weeks) Monday–Saturday, 10 A.M. to 5 P.M.; Sunday, noon to 5 P.M.; (Labor Day to Memorial Day) Wednesday–Saturday, 10 A.M. to 5 P.M.; Sunday, noon to 5 P.M.

Admissions: Under 1, free; all others, $5. First Friday of each month (5 P.M. to 8 P.M. is free to all. Parking garage 1½ blocks from museum — ticket validated at museum. Member ASTC.

For further information write to The Children's Museum of Maine, P.O. Box 4041, Portland, Maine 04101, or call (207) 828-1234 Ext. 001.

Maryland

Maryland Science Center
Baltimore, Maryland

The Maryland Science Center is a private, non-profit museum which features hundreds of hands-on activities, live demonstrations, and interactive displays, an IMAX Theater, and the Davis Planetarium in its three-story facility. The main exhibit galleries offer exhibits such as "Chesapeake Bay,"

"Experiment" (interactive activities for all ages), "Science Arcade" (more hands-on experiments), Van de Graaff Electrostatic Generator, "Energy," a Hubble Space Telescope, K.I.D.S. Room for 3–7 year olds, and more.

A 97-member staff works along with several hundred volunteers to keep the exhibits up to date and relevant to children today. Various demonstrations and events are also offered throughout the year.

Info in brief: A large, hands-on, interactive museum for children and their caregivers.

Location: Southwest corner of Baltimore's Inner Harbor.

Hours: Open every day except Thanksgiving and Christmas.

Admissions: Children, $7; adults, $9; seniors, $7. Member ASTC

Other sites of interest nearby: The many historic sites in Baltimore.

For further information write to the Maryland Science Center, 601 Light St., Baltimore, Maryland 21230-3812, or call (410) 685-5225 (24-hr. info line) or (410) 545-5964.

Rose Hill Manor
Children's Museum & Historic Park
Frederick, Maryland

Built in the 1790s, Rose Hill Manor was the retirement home of Maryland's first elected governor, Thomas Johnson. Johnson had earlier nominated George Washington as commander-in-chief of the Continental Army. The manor was the center of social activity in the area for many years around the turn of the century.

Opened in 1972 as a 43-acre children's museum and park, costumed guides now conduct tours through exhibits which include the 200-year-old manor house; icehouse; smokehouse; herb, vegetable and rose garden; orchard; log cabin; blacksmith shop; and carriage collection. A Farm Museum tour is also available.

The manor is now divided into two sections. Downstairs is the Children's Museum, which offers more than 300 items for children to "explore." After an introduction by the tour guide, children are allowed to play and learn while taking stitches on a quilt, carding wool, playing with replica toys and costumes, and operating a beaten biscuit machine, food chopper, and cream separator. Upstairs, visitors can see historic furnishings in a study, master bedroom, children's bedroom and domestic quarters outfitted with furniture and accessories of that period.

Various activities and special events provide visitors of all ages with an educational hands-on and visual experience.

Rose Hill Manor.

Info in brief: Hands-on experiences for children, along with village museum types of exhibits of interest to the entire family.

Location: Downtown Frederick, approximately 50 miles north of Washington, D.C.

Hours: April–October — Monday–Saturday, 10 A.M. to 4 P.M.; Sunday, 1 P.M. to 4 P.M.; November — weekends only; group reservations available year round.

Admissions: Contact museum for current admissions fees.

Unique exhibitions: The combination of historical displays and hands-on exhibits offers a unique way for visitors to learn about and experience history in motion.

Other sites of interest nearby: Washington, D.C., attractions, Ceresville Mansion, four national battlefields (Monocacy, Antietam, Harpers Ferry, and Gettysburg National Military Park/National Cemetery), Catoctin Mountain Zoological Park, Lilypons Water Gardens, several historic churches, historic landmarks, and other historic sites. (Be sure to contact the Tourism Council of Frederick County, Inc., at 1-800-999-3613 or 301-663-8687 for tour map and information.)

For further information write to Children's Museum, Rose Hill Manor Park, 1611 N. Market Street, Frederick, Maryland 21701-4304, or call (301) 694-1648.

Massachusetts

The Children's Museum
Boston, Massachusetts

Exhibits at The Children's Museum in Boston target children from pre-school age to teens. Two popular exhibits are El Mercado del Barrio (a kid-size neighborhood market) and Teen Tokyo, where visitors can even try sumo wrestling.

For further information write to The Children's Museum, 300 Congress St., Boston, Massachusetts.

Children's Museum
Holyoke, Massachusetts

At the time of this publication, the Children's Museum in Holyoke was undergoing major on-site construction, so contact the museum for updated information. Continuing exhibits include: Paperworks, where visitors make their own paper; Cityscape, a downtown city street role-play area; and Tot-Lot, for preschoolers. New exhibits planned include: "Do Something Constructive," an interactive building site; "CMTV-40," television studio; "The Body Playground," a health and well-being center.

Info in brief: A hands-on museum for children and their caregivers. Undergoing major construction at time of publication, so contact the museum for current information about exhibits.

Hours: Tuesday–Saturday, 9:30 A.M. to 4:30 P.M.; Sunday, noon to 5 P.M.

Admissions: $3 per visitor; seniors, $2.50. Memberships available.

For further information write to the Children's Museum, 444 Dwight St. at Heritage Park, Holyoke, Massachusetts 01040-5842, or call (413) 536-7048.

The Children's Museum in Easton
North Easton, Massachusetts

The Children's Museum in Easton is a small hands-on museum. Children can climb a firepole and ring a bell, roar with dinosaurs at the sand table, role-play at the Performance Center, use a giant kaleidoscope, zoom to the moon in the Moon Room, be a doctor in the Kidsclinic and more. Changing themes and exhibits, special classes and workshops and after-school programs are also offered throughout the year.

Info in brief: Small, hands-on, exploratory museum for young children and their caregivers.

Location: In Historic North Easton Village in the Old Fire Station, 9 Sullivan Avenue.

Hours: Tuesday–Saturday, 10 A.M. to 5 P.M.; Sunday, noon to 5 P.M. Open some Monday holidays.

Admissions: Under 2, free; all others, $3.50.

For further information write to The Children's Museum in Easton, P.O. Box 417, North Easton, Massachusetts 02356, or call (508) 230-3789.

Computer Museum
Boston, Massachusetts

The Computer Museum, with over 150 interactive exhibits, is the only museum in the world devoted to computers only, and to their impact on society.

Location: Museum Wharf.

Hours: (June–Labor Day) daily, 10 A.M. to 6 P.M. (September–May) Tuesday–Sunday, 10 A.M. to 5 P.M.

Admissions: Contact the museum for updated information.

Other sites of interest nearby: The many tourist attractions in Boston.

For further information write to the Computer Museum, Museum Wharf, 300 Congress St., Boston, Massachusetts 02114, or call (617) 423-6758.

Danforth Museum of Art
Framingham, Massachusetts

The Danforth Museum of Art is a contemporary art museum which features six galleries of 19th- and 20th-century American prints, drawings, paintings, photographs and sculptures. Hands-on activities for children are offered on a regular basis. Be sure to contact the museum for current information.

Hours: Wednesday–Sunday, noon to 5 P.M.

Admissions: Small admissions charge.

For further information write to the Danforth Museum of Art, 123 Union Ave., Framingham, Massachusetts, or call (508) 620-0060.

The Discovery Museums
Acton, Massachusetts

The Discovery Museums are actually two adjacent houses offering hands-on, interactive exhibits for children of all ages. The Children's Discovery Museum is housed in a 100-year-old Victorian home, and offers ten hands-on exhibit areas specifically for toddlers and preschoolers and their caregivers. The Science Discovery Museum is in the second house and offers creative challenging interactive, hands-on experiences with basic science and math themes for older children.

The Children's Discovery Museum opened in 1981 in a three-story, 3,500 sq. ft. building, emphasizing "learning through play." The Science Discovery Museum opened in 1987 and is now an award-winning museum, with 8,500

Outside musical special at the Discovery Museums in Acton, Massachusetts.

sq. ft. of space dedicated to the sciences and math for older children (basically 6 years through the teens).

Info in brief: Two adjacent houses filled with hands-on, interactive exhibits.

Hours: (School year) Tuesday, Thursday, and Friday, 1 P.M. to 4:30 P.M.; Wednesday, 9 A.M. to 6 P.M.; Saturday and Sunday, 9 A.M. to 4:30 P.M. (Summer) Tuesday–Sunday, 9 A.M. to 4:30 P.M.

Admissions: $6 per person per museum; $9 both museums the same day.

Other sites of interest nearby: Boston tourist attractions, including 34 museums.

For further information write to The Discovery Museums, 177 Main Street, Acton, Massachusetts 01720, or call (508) 264-4200. Web site: http://www/ ultranet.com/~discover/.

Hull Lifesaving Museum
Hull, Massachusetts

Although primarily a special-interest collections museum, the Hull Lifesaving Museum offers hands-on learning activities for children. An 1889 U.S. Life Saving Station has been furnished and equipped as a living museum about Boston harbor shipwreck rescues. Besides the hands-on exhibits, visitors can see the surfboat "Nantasket," a watchtower, a lighthouse display and can participate in rowing programs.

Info in brief: A collections museum with some hands-on activities for children.

Hours: (Late June–Labor Day) Wednesday–Sunday, noon to 5 P.M. (Labor Day–late June) Saturday and Sunday plus Monday holidays and school vacations, noon to 5 P.M.

Other sites of interest nearby: The many tourist attractions of nearby Boston.

For further information write to the Hull Lifesaving Museum, 1117 Nantasket Ave., Hull, Massachusetts, or call (617) 925-LIFE.

MIT Museum
Cambridge, Massachusetts

The MIT Museum offers visitors of all ages the chance to explore fascinating new technologies. Among other exhibits, visitors can create intricate mathematical structures and experiment to see how art and science are related.

Info in brief: A technical science museum with some hands-on exhibits for children.

Hours: Tuesday–Friday, 9 A.M. to 5 P.M.; Saturday and Sunday, noon to 5 P.M.

Other sites of interest nearby: Sports Museum of New England, USS *Constitution* Museum, Paul Revere House, New England Aquarium, Museum of Our National Heritage, Museum of Science (Boston), Children's Museum (Boston), Computer Museum, Danforth Museum of Art, Discovery Museums (Acton), and many more tourist attractions in Boston and the surrounding areas.

For further information write to MIT Museum, 265 Massachusetts Ave., Cambridge, Massachusetts, or call (617) 253-4444.

Museum of Our National Heritage
Lexington, Massachusetts

The Museum of Our National Heritage is an American History museum which features changing exhibits, including decorative arts, folk art, toys, famous Americans, and more. Although no permanent hands-on exhibits are on display, hands-on activities are offered by the museum frequently.

Hours: Monday–Saturday, 10 A.M. to 5 P.M.

Admissions: Free.

For further information write to the Museum of Our National Heritage, 33 Marrett Road, Lexington, Massachusetts, or call (617) 861-6559 or 861-0729.

Museum of Science
Boston, Massachusetts

The Museum of Science in Boston is a hands-on, exploratory museum for children with over 450 interactive exhibits on display.

Location: Science Park in Boston.

Hours: (Winter) Saturday–Thursday, 9 A.M. to 5 P.M.; Friday, 9 A.M. to 9 P.M.; (summer) Saturday–Thursday, 9 A.M. to 7 P.M.; Friday, 9 A.M. to 9 P.M.

Admissions: Member ASTC.

Other sites of interest nearby: Children's Museum on Congress St., Sports Museum of New England, USS *Constitution* Museum, Charles River Museum of Industry, Computer Museum on Museum Wharf, Discovery Museum on Main Street and more.

For further information write to the Museum of Science, Science Park, Boston, Massachusetts 02114-1099, or call (617) 723-2400.

New England Science Center
Worcester, Massachusetts

The primary target audience of the New England Science Center is families. It is an environmental museum whose aim is to use natural history collections, astronomy, living wildlife, cutting-edge technology and informations systems, and an extensive natural grounds area to encourage visitors to learn to live in and care for our natural environment. Events such as lectures, film series, and a jazz concert series are aimed at adults, but the museum does offer a "Discovery Room" for preschoolers and a special preschool day each month. A narrow-gauge railroad and the wildlife also attract young visitors. The museum currently has a master plan for expanding and updating facilities for the new millenium.

Info in brief: An environmental education center with a few hands-on activities for preschoolers. Wildlife opportunities are also available.

Location: About 40 minutes east of Springfield and about 45 minutes west of Boston.

Chinchillas up close at the New England Science Center (PHOTO COURTESY J.P. LANG-LANDS).

Hours: Monday–Saturday, 10 A.M. to 5 P.M.; Sunday, noon to 5 P.M. Closed some holidays.

Admissions: Under 3, free; children (3–16), $4; college students (with ID), $4; adults, $6; seniors, $4. Planetarium shows, $2. Train rides, $1.50. Member ASTC.

Unique features: The museum stems from one of the oldest natural history societies in America and has kept all of those collections.

Other sites of interest nearby: The Worcester Art Museum, Higgins Armory Museum, several Massachusetts Audubon Society sanctuaries, and many historic sites within the Blackstone River Valley National Heritage Corridor (birthplace of the American Industrial Revolution); Roger Williams Zoo (in Providence) and the Basketball Hall of Fame (in Springfield).

For further information write to the New England Science Center, 222 Harrington Way, Worcester, Massachusetts 01604, or call (508) 791-9211 or FAX (508) 791-6879. E-mail: lmyers@nesc.org.

The Sports Museum of New England
Boston, Massachusetts

The Sports Museum was in the process of relocating at the time of this writing. No definite location had been announced, but plans should be completed by 1998.

For further information write to The Sports Museum of New England, 1175 Soldiers Field Road, Boston, Massachusetts 02134, or call (617) 787-7678.

Michigan

Alfred P. Sloan Museum
Flint, Michigan

The Sloan Museum chronicles Flint's dramatic history as the birthplace of General Motors. Basically a historical museum, the Sloan Museum recently added a hands-on children's discovery center, offering permanent exhibits, changing exhibitions and special events throughout the year.

Info in brief: A historical, collections-type museum with one special center designated as a hands-on "Discovery Center" for children.

Hours: Monday–Friday, 10 A.M. to 5 P.M.; Saturday and Sunday, noon to 5 P.M.

Admissions: Contact the museum for updated information. Member ASTC.

Unique exhibits: The history of General Motors is extensive.

Other sites of interest nearby: Crossroads Village & Huckleberry Railroad, The (Flint) Children's Museum, Flint Institute of Arts, Junction Valley Railroad, and many other tourist attractions in Flint and the surrounding areas.

For further information write to Alfred P. Sloan Museum, 1221 E. Kearsley St., Flint, Michigan 48503, or call (810) 760-1169.

The Ann Arbor Hands-On Museum
Ann Arbor, Michigan

The Ann Arbor Hands-On Museum was conceived in 1978. It took four years to renovate the city's historic landmark firehouse and convert it into a museum that officially opened in October of 1982 with only 25 exhibits. The facility has grown into an outstanding science center with over 250 participatory exhibits that teach about science, art and history. Over 500 volunteers work with the full-time staff members to offer programs that have won the museum several awards. Current plans call for even more expansions in the near future.

Currently, the museum offers four floors of exhibits, including: First floor — "The Subject is You," where visitors learn about our bodies; second floor — "The World Around You" and "The Discovery Room," where visitors learn about physics, structures, waves, energy, other cultures and nature; third floor — "Crane's Roost," where visitors can explore light and optics; and the fourth floor — "How Things Work," where visitors play with simple machines, computers, math games and puzzles. Traveling exhibitions, classes and workshops, weekend demonstrations and other special programs are also offered throughout the year.

Info in brief: A hands-on, exploratory museum for children through middle-school ages and their families.

Location: In Ann Arbor's Historic Landmark Firehouse.

Hours: Tuesday–Friday, 10 A.M. to 5:30 P.M.; Saturday, 10 A.M. to 5 P.M.; Sunday, 1 P.M. to 5 P.M. Closed Mondays and major holidays.

Admissions: Children and students, $2.50; adults, $4; seniors, $2.50. Memberships available. Member ASTC.

For further information write to The Ann Arbor Hands-On Museum, 219 E. Huron St., Ann Arbor, Michigan 48104, or call (313) 995-5439.

The Children's Museum
Flint, Michigan

Opened in 1986, the Flint Children's Museum is a "please touch" museum that offers hands-on experiences and programs for children 10 years and younger. More than 100 exhibits are offered, encouraging children to learn more about their world through the act of play. Main exhibit areas include: "Let's Pretend" (ride in a storybook coach, shop, drive a fire engine, etc.); "Be Creative" (block building barn, lego table, magnets, and more); "It's Unbelievable" (bubbles, "anti-gravity" mirror, phosphorous wall, floor tile maze and more); and "Outrageously Artful" (wall of murals, art activity room, and more).

Special programs are also offered, and children get to meet "Stuffee," a life-size stuffed doll that helps visitors learn about the human body.

Info in brief: A hands-on arts and humanities museum for children 10 years and younger.

Hours: Monday–Saturday, 10 A.M. to 5 P.M.; Sunday, noon to 5 P.M. Closed major holidays.

Admissions: Under 2, free; children (2–12), $2.50; adults, $3; seniors, $2. Group and family rates available. Memberships available. Member ASTC.

Other sites of interest nearby: Crossroads Village & Huckleberry Railroad, Alfred P. Sloan Museum, Flint Institute of Arts, Junction Valley Railroad, and many other tourist attractions in Flint and the surrounding areas.

For further information write to The Children's Museum, 1602 W. Third Ave., Flint, Michigan 45804, or call (810) 767-KIDS (5437).

Curious Kids' Museum
St. Joseph, Michigan

An interactive hands-on museum which allows children to explore science, history and culture. Areas of exploration include "The Global Child" (life experiences around the world, including language, costumes, face painting, woodworking, puppets, and more); "Awesome Apples," "The Rain Forest," "Kids Port," "Machines," "Sound," "Body Works," and "Science Gallery." Besides the regular museum hours, special interest classes are held throughout the year. All classes are taught by trained teachers and scientists.

Info in brief: Hands-on participatory exhibits.

Location: Downtown St. Joseph on the bluff overlooking Lake Michigan.

Hours: (Mid-September to end of May) Wednesday, 10 A.M. to 8 P.M.; Thursday–Saturday, 10 A.M. to 5 P.M.; Sunday, noon to 5 P.M. (June–Sunday of Labor Day) same as previous schedule, but add Tuesday, 10 A.M. to 5 P.M.; after July 4, add Monday, 10 A.M. to 5 P.M. Closed during major holidays and Labor Day to mid-September.

Admissions: Under 2, free; ages 2 to adults, $3.

Other sites of interest nearby: The beaches of Lake Michigan.

For further information write to Curious Kids' Museum, 415 Lake Boulevard, St. Joseph, Michigan 49085, or call (616) 983-CKID (2543).

Impression 5 Science Museum
Lansing, Michigan

For further information contact: Impression 5 Science Museum, 200 Museum Dr., Lansing, Michigan 48933-1912, phone: (517) 485-8116. Member ASTC.

Minnesota

Headwaters Environmental Learning Center
Bemidji, Minnesota

The Headwaters Environmental Learning Center opened in March of 1994 and is a science- and nature-oriented museum located in downtown Bemidji. Some of the exhibits offered include: "Frozen Shadows," a darkroom with a strobe light; "Pitching Cage," which measures the velocity of a pitched ball; "Bubble Race"; a Bernouli Ball; "Symmetrigraph," a large apparatus that creates spirograph-type pictures; "Whisper Dishes"; "Laser Spirograph"; a small Hot Air Balloon; "Mirror Kaleidoscope"; and more. Several programs and demonstrations are also offered throughout the week.

Info in brief: A hands-on, interactive science museum for all members of the family, but of special interest to children.

Location: Downtown Bemidji, one block from Lake Bemidji.

Hours: Monday–Saturday, 9:30 A.M. to 5:30 P.M.; Sunday, 1 P.M. to 5 P.M.

Admissions: Under 12, $2; all others, $3. Memberships available. Member ASTC.

For further information write to Headwaters Science Center, 413 Beltrami Ave., Bemidji, Minnesota 56601, or call (218) 751-1110.

Laura Ingalls Wilder
Museum & Tourist Center
Walnut Grove, Minnesota

Although not strictly a hands-on interactive area for children, this museum is included in this book because of its special appeal to children. For several generations children (and adults) have been fascinated by the "Little House on the Prairie" books and TV series. Memorabilia from Wilder's life and from the TV series are seen here.

Included in the exhibits are a quilt made by Laura and her daughter, a Bible from the Ingalls' church, scale models of the Ingalls' farm and TV series homes, historic documents, memorabilia of visits by "Little House" TV stars, the Kelton Doll Collection and much more. The museum's collections are housed in several buildings on the grounds, most dating from the late 1800s.

Info in brief: A type of village museum of interest to all ages, but with special interest to children.

Hours: Memorial Day–Labor Day, 10 A.M. to 7 P.M.; May and September, 10 A.M. to 5 P.M.; April and October, 10 A.M. to 3 P.M.; appointments available.

Admissions: $2 per person.

Other sites of interest nearby: Mankato & N. Mankato (Minnesota's other Twin Cities), Minneopa State Park, New Ulm (an old German city), the town of Sleepy Eye, Petroglyphs, Lower Sioux Agency, Pipestone Monument and more.

For further information write to the Laura Ingalls Wilder Museum & Tourist Center, Box 58, Walnut Grove, Minnesota 56180, or call 1-800-761-1009, (507) 859-2358 or 859-2155.

Minnesota Children's Museum
St. Paul, Minnesota

Opened in 1995, the Minnesota Children's Museum is an interactive museum which encourages families to come and explore their world together through the arts, sciences and humanities. Children ages six months to 12 years are targeted in the hands-on exhibits and various programs. The six main galleries are called "One World," "World Works," "Habitot," "Earth World," "Changing World," and "World of Wonder." In the galleries, children are encouraged to crawl through a giant anthill, operate a crane, clamber up a musical sculpture, and more. Changing exhibits are also offered periodically. A daily reading time, special Bedtime Thursday Night reading time and book swaps are part of the program the museum has initiated to encourage reading in the community.

Info in brief: Hands-on, interactive museum for children 12 years and younger and their families.

Location: One of the buildings in the complex of the World Trade Center in downtown St. Paul at the intersection of 7th and Wabasha streets.

Hours: Tuesday, Wednesday, Friday–Sunday, 9 A.M. to 5 P.M.; Thursday, 9 A.M. to 8 P.M.; (Memorial Day–Labor Day and holidays) also open Monday, 9 A.M. to 5 P.M. Closed Thanksgiving and Christmas.

Admissions: Under 1, free; toddlers (1 & 2), $3.95; age 3–Adult, $5.95; seniors (60+), $3.95. Memberships available.

Other sites of interest nearby: World Trade Center, Science Museum of Minnesota, Rice Park/Cultural District, Union Depot Place, Town Square entertainment complex, State Capitol buildings, and the Valleyfair Amusement Park located in Shakopee (about 20 minutes away).

For further information write to Minnesota Children's Museum, 10 W. 7th St., St. Paul, Minnesota 55102, or call (612) 225-6000.

Runestone Museum
Alexandria, Minnesota

The Runestone Museum is named for the Kensington Runestone, a large stone with Runic writing carved on it, dating back to 1362. It was carved and left by Viking explorers who came from a settlement called Vinland in Nova Scotia. Vinland was the area of North America discovered by Leif Eriksson around A.D. 1000.

Other display areas include the Alexandria Room, featuring items from the 1800s specifically used in the area, a small theater showing a video about the Vikings and the Runestone, a Minnesota Wildlife area and an outside area called Fort Alexandria. This area enables visitors to see an actual fort built in 1863 due to the unrest between the Sioux Indians and the area settlers. In the fort are an authentic local area one-room schoolhouse with original artifacts, an old log cabin, a general store, a one-room church, and an agricultural building which features antique farm machinery, a rare old snowmobile, a doctor's office and other artifacts.

Although the museum is not an official children's museum, the managers say that the exhibits are displayed "with the intent of as much hands-on orientation as possible."

Info in brief: A small tourist attraction–type museum with opportunities for hands-on experiences.

Hours: Monday–Friday, 9 A.M. to 5 P.M.; Saturday, 11 A.M. to 4 P.M. (Summer: 9 A.M. to 5 P.M.); Sunday, noon to 5 P.M. (Summers only).

Admissions: Adults, $4; seniors, $3; youth, $2; under 6, free.

Other sites of interest nearby: The Budd Car/North Shore Scenic Railroad in Duluth, Duluth-Lakefront Tour in Duluth, Lake Superior & Mississippi Railroad in Duluth, Lake Superior Museum of Transportation in Duluth, Minnesota Transportation Museum in Stillwater, North Star Rail in Bloomington, Paul Bunyan Center in Brainerd, and the Valleyfair Amusement Park in Shakopee. The Canadian border is also nearby.

For further information write to Runestone Museum, 206 Broadway, Alexandria, Minnesota 56308, or call (612) 763-3160.

Science Museum of Minnesota
Minneapolis, Minnesota

The Science Museum of Minnesota features both natural history and technology. It has been a national leader in developing hands-on exhibits,

Omnitheater films, school outreach and youth science programs, and more. Current exhibits include: "Dinosaurs and Fossils"; "Green Street," with exhibits about energy use and conservation; "Anthropology Hall," exploring the world's cultures; and "Experiment Gallery" with hands-on experiments galore. Other features of the museum include the Youth Computer Center (one of the first nationwide), Warner Nature Center (a 600-acre nature preserve), and the Omnitheater (second one built in the country).

The museum is preparing for the new millennium, when a new, five-level Science Museum will open its doors. This new 350,000 sq. ft. facility will feature the latest Omnifilm technology, educational entertainment, outdoor activities at the Mississippi River, expanded and interconnected science halls indoors and out, a multi-acre nature center; discovery programs; hundreds of hands-on experiments, and a Youth Science Center for teens. Plans call for the opening to be in 1999.

Info in brief: A hands-on (and more) science museum for children of all ages and their caregivers.

Location: Off I-94 and I-35E on the corners of Exchange and Wabasha in downtown St. Paul, 15 minutes from the Mall of America or downtown Minneapolis.

Hours: (Museum) Monday–Saturday, 9:30 A.M. to 9 P.M.; Sunday, 10 A.M. to 9 P.M. (Omnitheater show times) Monday–Friday, 2, 3, 7, 8 P.M. and 9 P.M. on Friday; Saturday and Sunday, 11 A.M., noon, 1, 2, 3, 4, 7, 8 P.M. and 10 A.M. and 9 P.M. on Saturday.

Admissions: Under 4, free. (Omnitheater/exhibits) children (4–15), $6; adults, $8; seniors (65+), $6. (Omnitheater only) children, $5; adults, $6; seniors, $5. (Exhibits only) children, $4; adults, $5; seniors, $4. (Omnifest) purchase a combination Omnitheater and exhibit hall ticket to see one film. Additional films will cost $4 each. Member ASTC.

Other sites of interest nearby: Paul Bunyan Center (Brainerd), Valleyfair Amusement Park (Shakopee), and the Ramsey & Dakota County Historical Tours (railroad).

For further information write to the Science Museum of Minnesota, 30 East Tenth St., St. Paul, Minnesota 55101, or call (612) 221-9444 (TDD 221-4585) or FAX (612) 221-4777.

Missouri

American Royal Museum
American Royal Association
Kansas City, Missouri

The American Royal Association is sponsor of the American Royal Livestock, Horse Show and Rodeo. The American Royal Museum is another facet of the Association, offering three main exhibit areas: "History," "The American Royal" (a livestock horse show/rodeo), and "Hands-On" (exploratory museum for children).

In the hands-on area, children can judge livestock and compare their scores with professional judges, weigh themselves on a real Fairbanks livestock scale, grind wheat, learn about milling, use microscopes (to inspect hides, hooves, bones, and more), dress up in Western and English riding attire, sit on saddles and see themselves in the ring, play with puppets in the barn area, visit a mini theater showing rodeo and horseshow vignettes, see movies about the American Royal and agriculture, and play computer games such as The Oregon Trail and Ag Ease. Docents are available if needed, or visitors can explore the museum and some of its facilities on their own.

Info in brief: A hands-on museum for children, with other areas more of interest to adults. Targeted audience would be families especially interested in livestock, horses and other agricultural pursuits, as well as families with an interest in the American West and history.

Hours: Tuesday–Friday, 10 A.M. to 4 P.M.; Saturday and Sunday, by appointment only. Open some weekends for special events. Be sure to contact the Association for current information.

Admissions: Children (2–12), $2; adults, $4; seniors, FFA, other groups, $2.50.

Unique exhibits: Unique theme of livestock, and agriculture, chronicling the history of Kansas City and America's move West.

Other sites of interest nearby: Oceans of Fun Water Park, Worlds of Fun Amusement Park, and other Kansas City tourist attractions.

For further information write to the American Royal Association & Visitors Center, 1701 American Royal Court, Kansas City, Missouri 64102, or call (816) 221-9800 or FAX (816) 221-8189.

Kaleidoscope
Hallmark Visitors Center
Kansas City, Missouri

Kaleidoscope is a participatory arts program for children ages 5 to 12. This program occurs at the Hallmark Square at Crown Center in Kansas City at Hallmark's international headquarters. At this site is the Kaleidoscope permanent exhibit showcasing Hallmark's historic and artistic development.

Kaleidoscope began in 1969 as a traveling exhibition, and outreach programs still exist, but the permanent exhibit was opened at Crown Center in 1975 and serves approximately 83,000 children per year. Programs are held on Saturdays, with four 55-minute sessions offered each day. Kaleidoscope is free, but tickets must be obtained in the lobby, beginning about 10 A.M. each morning. Tickets are distributed on a first-come, first-served basis and are given to children ages 5 to 12 only. Large groups need to make reservations. Weekday sessions are also offered, but visitors must contact Kaleidoscope for a current schedule and up-to-date information.

Kaleidoscope's participatory arts program is for children only. Adults are not allowed in the sessions, but can watch through observation windows or volunteer to be helpers for the entire group. All materials used are scrap materials from Hallmark manufacturing. Children are encouraged to be creative with these materials, without fear of criticism or failure.

Info in brief: A hands-on participatory program located in a collections museum (Hallmark).

Location: At Crown Center, outside of the third level of Halls, next to the Hallmark Visitors Center.

Hours: Saturday sessions: 10:30 A.M., noon, 1:15 P.M., and 2:30 P.M. Summer weekday sessions are also offered. Contact Kaleidoscope for up-to-date information. Hallmark Visitors Center — Monday–Friday, 9 A.M. to 5 P.M.; Saturday, 9:30 A.M. to 4:30 P.M. Call for holiday hours.

Admissions: Free to both the Visitors Center and Kaleidoscope.

Unique exhibits: Visitors Center is a museum dedicated to a collection of Hallmark memorabilia.

Other sites of interest nearby: The Toy and Miniature Museum of Kansas City, Kansas Cosmosphere & Space Center, Kansas City Museum, Jesse James historic sites, Kansas City Zoo, NCAA Hall of Champions, Nelson-Atkins Museum of Art, Auto Museum, American Royal Museum & Visitors Center, and other Kansas City tourist attractions.

For further information write to Kaleidoscope, Hallmark Square at Crown Center, P.O. Box 419580, Kansas City, Missouri 64141-6580, or call (816) 274-8300 or 8301.

Kansas City Museum
Kansas City, Missouri

The Kansas City Museum is housed in the former Robert A. Long Mansion, "Corinthian Hall," in Kansas City's historic northeast neighborhood. The museum displays regional history (both cultural and natural), a hands-on weather exhibit, a planetarium, and Challenger Learning Center space flight simulator. Live science demonstrations are also offered every Saturday during the school year.

Info in brief: A family museum with hands-on activities for children, plus availability of a space flight simulator and planetarium shows.

Location: In Kansas City's historic northeast neighborhood.

Hours: Tuesday–Saturday, 9:30 A.M. to 4:30 P.M.; Sunday, noon to 4:30 P.M. Contact museum for up-to-date schedules for planetarium showtimes and flight simulator rides.

Admissions: Under 3, free; children (3–17), $2; adults, $2.50; seniors, $2. Planetarium and Challenger (flight simulator)—additional charges. Member ASTC.

Unique features: The museum is creating a new science center, "Science City," inside Kansas City's historic Union Station. This will be a hands-on science center for children and their families. No definite opening date was given at the time of this writing, but be sure to contact the Kansas City Museum for further information.

Other sites of interest nearby: Kaleidoscope, Toy and Miniature Museum, Jesse James historic sites, Kansas City Zoo, NCAA Hall of Champions, American Royal Museum & Visitors Center, Kansas Cosmosphere & Space Center, and other Kansas City attractions.

For further information write to the Kansas City Museum, 3218 Gladstone Blvd., Kansas City, Missouri 64123, or call (816) 483-8300.

The Magic House
St. Louis Children's Museum
St. Louis, Missouri

According to their research, The Magic House in Kirkwood in St. Louis is the third most popular children's museum in the United States. This hands-on museum is partially housed in a Victorian mansion built in 1901 as a private home for the George Lane Edwards family. After serious renovations, The Magic House opened to the public in October of 1979 operating solely on admissions fees. In 1985, a 2,000 sq. ft. exhibition area for children ages 1–7 was added, with exhibits encouraging the enhancement of gross motor skills, self-concept and self-esteem. In 1987, "The Gallery" opened with a collection that explores the relationship between art and modern technology. Today, more than 70 hands-on exhibits are offered for children of all ages. Special events, outreach programs and workshops are also offered. At the time of this writing, the museum had plans for an expansion program that would double the size of the museum. Projected plans called for a late 1997 opening date — contact the museum for current information.

Info in brief: Large participatory museum for children of all ages.

Location: One mile north of I-44 on Lindbergh Blvd.

Hours: (School year) Tuesday–Thursday, 1 P.M. to 5:30 P.M.; Friday, 1 P.M. to

9 P.M.; Saturday, 9:30 A.M. to 5:30 P.M.; Sunday, 11:30 A.M. to 5:30 P.M. (Summer) Tuesday–Thursday and Saturday, 9:30 A.M. to 5:30 P.M.; Friday, 9:30 A.M. to 9 P.M.; Sunday, 11:30 A.M. to 5:30 P.M.

Admissions: Adults and children, $3.50; seniors, $2.50. Member of AYM.

Other sites of interest nearby: St. Louis Gateway Arch, the St. Louis Zoo, Six Flags Over Mid-America and other St. Louis tourist attractions.

For further information write to The Magic House, St. Louis Children's Museum, 516 S. Kirkwood Rd. (Lindbergh Blvd.), St. Louis, Missouri 63122, or call (314) 822-8900.

St. Louis Science Center
St. Louis, Missouri

The St. Louis Science Center is a complex of three buildings which feature more than 650 exhibits on ecology and environment, aviation, technology, human adventure and space sciences. Exhibits include life-size, animated dinosaurs, an underground tunnel, and 24 outdoor playground-type exhibits. An Omnimax Theater shows films on a four-story domed screen and a

St. Louis Science Center.

planetarium features high-tech star shows and laser shows. Traveling exhibitions are also offered twice each year.

Info in brief: A hands-on, interactive and exploratory museum for children and their caregivers.

Location: Just west of Kings Highway, off I-64.

Hours: Monday–Thursday, 9 A.M. to 5 P.M.; Friday, 9 A.M. to 9 P.M.; Saturday, 10 A.M. to 9 P.M.; Sunday, 11 A.M. to 6 P.M.

Admissions: Free. Nominal charges for theaters, Discovery Room and some traveling exhibitions. Member ASTC.

Other sites of interest nearby: The many tourist attractions in St. Louis.

For further information write to the St. Louis Science Center, 5050 Oakland Ave., St. Louis, Missouri 63110, or call 1-800-456-SLSC or (314) 289-4444 or 289-4419 or FAX (314) 533-8687. Website: www.slsc.org. E-mail: bpharms@slsc.org.

Science City at Union Station
Kansas City, Missouri

Science City is a new hands-on museum being created by the Kansas City Museum. Visitors will be able to explore prehistoric Kansas City, broadcast from the television station, and participate in numerous hands-on science explorations.

An exact opening date was not available at the time of this writing, but the museum and the Union Station Assistance Corporation are working together to restore Union Station and to create a new state-of-the-art science and technology center for children.

Location: In Kansas City's historic Union Station.

For further information write to the Kansas City Museum, 3218 Gladstone Blvd., Kansas City, Missouri 64123, or call (816) 483-8300.

The Toy and Miniature Museum of Kansas City
Kansas City, Missouri

Although The Toy and Miniature Museum is not a hands-on museum, the content of the collections is of much interest to children. It is the only museum of its kind in the Midwest and is considered to be one of the best in the world. At the museum, visitors find miniatures, toys, dolls and doll houses dating from the 19th century to the present day. All miniatures have been reduced to an exact scale and represent an historically correct replica of the original — most of which actually work. The Toys and Dolls exhibits help teach children about past generations and their surroundings. The doll houses in this collection range in date from the early 1800s to the mid–20th century.

Besides the regular exhibits, puppet shows and other special events for children are offered throughout the year. Holiday events are especially festive. Contact the museum for an updated schedule.

After opening several years ago in an elegant and historic Kansas City mansion, a renovation plan and addition were finally completed in 1989, bringing the total exhibit space up to over 21,000 sq. ft. The mansion/museum actually sits on the University of Missouri–Kansas City campus.

Info in brief: A collections-type museum whose content is of special interest to children.

Location: University of Missouri–Kansas City campus.

Hours: Wednesday–Saturday, 10 A.M. to 4 P.M.; Sunday, 1 P.M. to 4 P.M. Closed Monday and Tuesday, major holidays and annually the first two weeks in September.

Admissions: Children, $2; adults, $4; seniors/students, $3.50.

Other sites of interest nearby: Kaleidoscope, Jesse James historic sites, Kansas City Zoo, NCAA Hall of Champions, American Royal Museum & Visitors Center, Kansas Cosmosphere & Space Center, and other Kansas City attractions.

For further information write to The Toy & Miniature Museum of Kansas City, 5235 Oak St., Kansas City, Missouri 64112, or call (816) 333-2055.

Nebraska

Edgerton Explorit Center
Aurora, Nebraska

The mission of the Edgerton Explorit Center is to feature and expand on the work of Dr. Harold Edgerton of MIT, who is probably most famous for his stop-action photography and the invention of the strobe light. The museum hopes to nurture in people Dr. Edgerton's joy of learning by creating hands-on learning experiences for people of all ages and backgrounds. Several full-time staff members, one "Scientist in Residence" and more than 40 regular volunteers work to instill this love of learning in all visitors.

The 12,000 sq. ft. building includes a rotunda, classroom, theater/lecture hall, main exhibit hall, offices and shop area. The Plainsman Museum is adjoining, connected by "strobe alley," a duplication of the area outside Edgerton's MIT office. Eighteen major exhibit areas are offered in the exhibit galleries, while in-house education programs, traveling exhibits and programs, historical preservation, special events, and educational products and exhibit development are also emphasized.

Info in brief: A hands-on science museum for children and their caregivers.

Location: 1 hour west of Lincoln, Nebraska on I-80 and 3 miles north of the I-80 Aurora exit. The Plainsman Museum is adjoining.

Hours: (Summer) Monday–Saturday, 9 A.M. to 5 P.M.; Sunday, 1 P.M. to 5 P.M. Closed holidays. (Winter) Tuesday–Saturday, 10 A.M. to 5 P.M.; Sunday, 1 P.M. to 5 P.M.; Closed Monday and holidays.

Admissions: School-age children, $2.50; adults, $3.50. Member ASTC.

Other sites of interest nearby: The Plainsman Museum, Courthouse Square (historic downtown area), and several historic homes open for viewing.

For further information write to Edgerton Explorit Center, 208 16th St., Aurora, Nebraska 68818 or call (402) 694-4032. Website: http://www.hamilton.net/aurora/city/edgerton.htm. E-mail: (edgerton@hamilton.net).

Lincoln Children's Museum
Lincoln, Nebraska

The Lincoln Children's Museum first opened in 1989, moving to its current location in the fall of 1991. The five full-time and 11 part-time staff, along with several hundred volunteers, encourage children, youth and adults to explore and discover their environment in this 15,524 sq. ft. space. The four main exhibit areas are: "Science/Technology Discovery Area," "History/Culture Area," "Toddler Area," and "Fine Arts Area." Other exhibits include the "Little Husker Stadium," "Bubbles," "Experiencing Agriculture," "Lunar Lander," "Recollections," "KIDS Radio station," "LCM Bank," "Super Market," "Celebrate Abilities" and more.

Info in brief: A growing, hands-on museum especially for children.

Location: In an historic building in the heart of downtown Lincoln.

Hours: Tuesday–Saturday, 10 A.M. to 5 P.M.; Sunday and Monday, 1 P.M. to 5 P.M.; closed Wednesday and most major holidays.

The Lunar Lander Exhibit at Lincoln Children's Museum.

Admissions: Under 2, free; all others, $3. Memberships available.

Unique exhibits: Celebrate Abilities — designed to create awareness of the basic needs of all humans, and to encourage a positive attitude toward people with disabilities.

Other sites of interest nearby: Nebraska State Capital, Sheldon Art Gallery, Lied Center for Performing Arts, Museum of Nebraska History, Morrill Hall Museum of Natural History, Kennard House and the entertainment and restaurant district of downtown Lincoln.

For further information write to Lincoln Children's Museum, Lincoln Square, 121 South 13th St., Suite 103, Lincoln, Nebraska 68508, or call (402) 477-0128 or 477-4000.

Omaha Children's Museum
Omaha, Nebraska

The Omaha Children's Museum celebrated its 20th anniversary in October 1996. Beginning as a portable "traveling" museum which basically operated out of the trunk of a car, the goal of the museum has always been to offer educational exhibits and activities of specific interest to children. Now housed in a permanent 60,000 sq. ft. building, the primary goal is still to educate and benefit children in the metropolitan community. Their stated purpose is to "provide high quality participatory and educational experiences, oriented to the interests of children, in the areas of the arts, humanities, and natural and applied sciences." More than 100,000 people participated in these experiences in 1995.

The layout of the museum offers 11 main areas of exploration, along with offices and restroom facilities. The areas include: Model of Omaha, Toddler Space, Legos/Giant Blocks, Face Paints, Temporary Exhibitions, Charlie Campbell Science & Technology Center, Creativity Center, Performance Area, Activity Rooms, Birthday Room and the OCM Museum Store.

Info in brief: Hands-on, participatory exhibits are emphasized. (All children must be accompanied and supervised by an adult.)

Location: 500 South 20th Street, Omaha, Nebraska.

Hours: Tuesday–Saturday, 10 A.M. to 5 P.M.; Sunday, 1 P.M. to 5 P.M. (Closed Monday and major holidays.)

Admissions: Age 2–adult, $4; seniors, $3; children under 2, free. Memberships are offered. Member ASTC.

Unique exhibits or exhibitions: Toddler Space (for those under 6 years of age).

Other sites of interest nearby: Joslyn Art Museum, Henry Doorly Zoo, Brandeis Building, Old Market, Western Heritage Museum, Omaha Theater Company for Young People, Great Plains Black Museum, Boys Town, Burlington Building, Central High School.

For further information write to the Omaha Children's Museum, 500 South 20th St., Omaha, Nebraska 68102, or call (402) 342-6164 or FAX (402) 342-6165. Website: www.ocm.org or E-mail to: discover@ocm.org.

Nevada

Guinness World of Records Museum
Las Vegas, Nevada

Although the Guinness World of Records Museum is not strictly a children's museum, the items on display are of definite interest to children (and their caregivers) around the world. With over 5,200 sq. ft. of exhibits, the

"The Oldest Man" exhibit at Las Vegas, Nevada's Guinness World of Records Museum.

museum brings "amazing feats" and "astonishing facts" to life in its three-dimensional displays. Visitors find exhibits, displays, rare videos, artifacts, computerized data banks, life-size replicas of famous people and much more.

Main theme areas are "The Human World," "The Animal World," "The World of Sports," "Space," "The Arts & Entertainment," "The World of Cinema," "The Natural World," and "The World of Las Vegas."

Info in brief: A visual museum with items of interest to most children.

Location: On the Strip one block north of the Circus Circus Hotel.

Hours: (September–May) daily, 9 A.M. to 6 P.M.; (June–August) daily, 9 A.M. to 8 P.M.

Admissions: Adults, $4.95; seniors, military and students, $3.95; children (5–12), $2.95; under 4, free. Group rates available.

Other sites of interest nearby: The many tourist attractions in Las Vegas.

For further information write to the Guinness World of Records Museum, 2780 Las Vegas Blvd. S., Las Vegas, Nevada 89109, or call (702) 792-3766 or FAX (702) 792-0530.

Lied Discovery Children's Museum
Las Vegas, Nevada

The Lied Discovery Children's Museum was founded in 1984 as a private, nonprofit educational institution. Several temporary exhibits were set up

Lied Discovery Children's Museum.

at different locations around the Las Vegas Valley in order to promote the idea of building a proper museum. A permanent home was finally opened for visitation in 1990, but ongoing plans call for continued growth and improvements.

The 22,000 sq. ft. (exhibit area) museum currently features over 100 hands-on exhibits in the arts, sciences and humanities. Special demonstrations, activities, and workshops are also offered throughout the year. Some of the permanent exhibits include "Toddler Towers" (crawl and slide), "Performing Arts Stage," a space shuttle, a gyrochair, color computers complete with printers, "Musical Pathway," a giant bubble machine, KKID radio and more.

Info in brief: A hands-on arts, sciences and humanities museum mainly for children ages 6–12 and their caregivers.

Location: Adjoining the Las Vegas Library.

Hours: (School year) Wednesday–Saturday, 10 A.M. to 5 P.M.; Sunday, noon to 5 P.M. Open most school holidays. (Summer — June, July, August) Tuesday–Saturday, 10 A.M. to 5 P.M.; Sunday, noon to 5 P.M.

Admissions: Under 2, free; children (3–11), $3; children (12+), $4; adults, $5; seniors and military, $4. Memberships available. Member ASTC.

Other sites of interest nearby: The many tourist attractions in Las Vegas. (Food and motel rates are especially low.)

For further information write to Lied Discovery Children's Museum, 833 Las Vegas Blvd. North, Las Vegas, Nevada 89101, or call (702) 382-3445 or FAX (702) 382-0592.

The Wilbur D. May Center
Reno, Nevada

The Wilbur D. May Center has three distinct areas — The Wilbur D. May Museum, The Great Basin Adventure and the May Arboretum. The museum is a collection of artifacts and trophies from around the world. It also hosts a variety of traveling exhibits throughout the year, including Dinamation, a science carnival, rain forest exhibit, computer exhibit and more. Visitors are given "treasure hunt" sheets upon entry, and are awarded a prize at the end of their visit if they find all the "treasures" while visiting the museum exhibits.

The May Arboretum is open to the public all day and offers special children's tours and family tours upon request.

While all three areas are family oriented, the Great Basin Adventure is of special interest to children. Included in this small theme park are pony

Zebra and African hunting implements in The Wilbur D. May Museum.

rides, a log flume ride, a dinosaur playground, gold panning, a petting zoo, a discovery room and a concession stand.

Info in brief: Small participatory theme park for children, as well as an arboretum and historical museum.

Location: A few miles from downtown Reno.

Hours: Vary according to the season. (Summer) Tuesday–Sunday, 10 A.M. to 5 P.M.; (Winter) Wednesday–Sunday, 10 A.M. to 5 P.M. Arboretum is open different hours. Contact the center before visiting.

Admissions: Small admissions fee.

Other sites of interest nearby: Reno, Nevada, attractions.

For further information write to The Wilbur D. May Center, Rancho San Rafael Park, 1502 Washington St., Reno, Nevada 89503, or call (702) 785-5961.

New Hampshire

The Children's Metamorphosis
Londonderry, New Hampshire

This two-story museum is a total hands-on museum for children between the ages of 1 and 8. Exploration areas include: "The Sticky Room," with magnets, a sticky mural, and snap blocks; "Emergency Room," where children can be patient or doctor; "The Waterplay Area"; "The Construction Site"; "The Rainbow Room," where children learn about color and light; "Dinosaur Times"; "Grammy's Attic"; "Puppet Theatre"; "Post Office"; "Nature Center"; "World Culture" and "Toddler Play." There is also a train and picnic area outside.

Group tours are available along with birthday parties, overnight programs and special events.

Info in brief: Hands-on, participatory children's museum.

Location: Route 28 exactly one mile north of Exit 5 off I-93 near Londonderry.

Hours: Tuesday, 9:30 A.M. to 5 P.M.; Sunday, 1 P.M. to 5 P.M.; Friday, 5 P.M. to 8 P.M. Also open Mondays of school vacations and July and August. Closed major holidays.

Admissions: Ages 1 through adult, $3.75. Friday evenings, $7 per family. (Children must always be accompanied by an adult.) Memberships are offered.

Other sites of interest nearby: The Stonyfield Farm Yogurt Works tours and Mack's Apples, a National Bicentennial Farm U-Pick and farm market.

For further information write to The Children's Metamorphosis, 217 Rockingham Road, Londonderry, New Hampshire 03053, or call (603) 425-2560.

The Children's Museum of Portsmouth
Portsmouth, New Hampshire

The Children's Museum of Portsmouth opened in 1983 after two years of planning. Since that time, expansions and new innovations have taken place so that the museum now features more than 16 hands-on theme exhibits to explore, along with special events, programs, workshops, etc. Ongoing exhibits include "Earthquakes Are Natural," "Different Lands, Different Masks,"

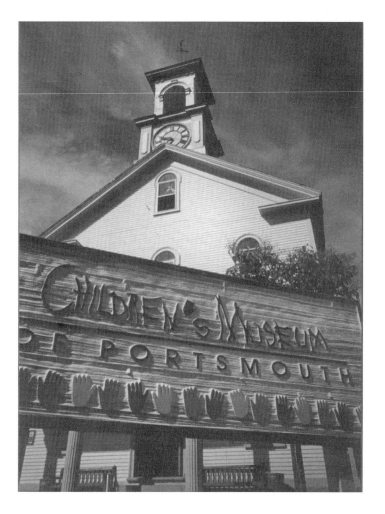

"Magicam," "Body Bits," "Lobstering," "Yellow Submarine" (a two-story play structure), "Siss Boom Bang" (music room), "Primary Place & Resource Center," "Forms of Expression," "Space Shuttle," and more. A project area and mini-exhibits are also on display.

The South Meeting House, which houses the museum, is listed on the National Register of Historic Places and is leased by the city to the museum for $1 a year. The 1863 building has been refurbished and transformed into the children's museum, but has managed to maintain its unique architectural features and historic charm.

Info in brief: A hands-on and interactive museum for children and their caregivers.

Hours: Tuesday–Saturday, 10 A.M. to 5 P.M.; Sunday, 1 P.M. to 5 P.M.; (during summer and school vacations) Monday, 10 A.M. to 5 P.M. Closed some holidays.

Admissions: Under 2, free; seniors, $3; children and adults, $4. Children under 12 must be accompanied by an adult.

For further information write to The Children's Museum of Portsmouth, 280 Marcy St., Portsmouth, New Hampshire 03801, or call (603) 436-3853 or FAX (603) 436-7706. Website: http://www.rscs.net/children/home.html.

New Hampshire Farm Museum
Milton, New Hampshire

The New Hampshire Farm Museum is a living history museum which allows children to participate in actual 1890s farm-related chores. Some of the chores visitors are allowed to experience include grooming and feeding the barn animals; harrowing, planting, cultivating and harvesting gardens; weaving; spinning; buttermaking; clotheswashing on a scrub board, and more. Although most tours are docent guided for school groups, several special events are held throughout the year, and all of these major events include similar hands-on activities. Groups of 15 or more may also book tours. Contact the museum before visiting in order to get a current calendar of special events. Some of these include workshops, concerts, barn dances, trailriding, Easter Egg Festival, Soup Taste and Hayride and more.

Info in brief: Living history museum which is not open to the general public except for special events or prearranged tours.

Location: On Route 125, Plummer's Ridge, in Milton (Exit 18 off the Spaulding Turnpike.)

Hours: 10 A.M. to 4 P.M.—(Mid-May through mid–June), weekends only; (mid–June through Labor Day) daily; (Labor Day to mid–October), weekends only.

Admissions: Under 3, free; children (3–12), $1.50; adults, $5. Concerts and some special events require additional charges. Memberships available.

Other sites of interest nearby: The White Mountains and the Atlantic Ocean. Many bed and breakfasts and resorts are in the area.

For further information write to the New Hampshire Farm Museum, P.O. Box 644, Milton, New Hampshire 03851, or call (603) 652-7840.

SEE Science Center
Manchester, New Hampshire

The SEE Science Center is a hands-on discovery center whose aim is to promote the understanding, enjoyment and achievements of science for visitors 4 years of age and older. More than 65 hands-on exhibits are offered along with workshops, seminars, overnighters, and outreach programs.

Major exhibits emphasize electricity, momentum and light. Visitors weighing less than 80 pounds can even experience moon-like conditions in the Moonwalk Exhibit.

Info in brief: Hands-on, participatory museum for children and their caregivers. Targeted audience given as 4 through adult.

Hours: (School year) Saturday and Sunday, noon to 5 P.M.; open to school groups during the week. (Summer and school vacation weeks) weekdays, 10 A.M. to 3 P.M.

Admissions: Under 3, free; all others, $3. Member ASTC.

Unique exhibits: Moonwalk Exhibit for visitors weighing less than 80 pounds.

Other sites of interest nearby: Anheuser Busch, Amoskeag Fishways, Christa McAuliffe Planetarium, and the Boston Museum of Science.

For further information write to SEE Science Center, 324 Commercial St., Manchester, New Hampshire 03101, or call or FAX (603) 669-0400. Web page: www.see-sciencecenter.org.

New Jersey

Bergen Museum of Art and Science
Paramus, New Jersey

The Bergen Museum is a large, two-story, family-oriented arts and sciences museum which offers exhibitions for all age ranges. A hands-on science area especially for children is one of the exhibits. The Mastodon skeleton collection, the Lenape Indian exhibit and the Nature Room are also of special interest for children, but are not hands-on. Other permanent collections include artwork by important artists of Northern New Jersey and Metropolitan New York, the Science in Art Collection, and an Ethnic Heritage Collection.

Many classes, workshops, concerts and special events for children are sponsored by the museum year round. A variety of visiting exhibits is also offered throughout the year, making it an ever-changing museum.

Info in brief: Arts and sciences museum with some areas specifically for children.

Location: Ridgewood and Fairview avenues in Paramus.

Hours: Tuesday–Saturday, 10 A.M. to 5 P.M.; Sunday, 1 P.M. to 5 P.M. Closed Monday.

Admissions: Fees vary according to tour chosen. Generally $2.50 to $4.

Unique exhibits: Mastodon collection and Lenape Indian exhibit.

Other sites of interest nearby: Clementon Lake Park (Clementon), Six Flags Great Adventure (Jackson).

For further information write to the Bergen Museum of Art and Science, 327 E. Ridgewood Ave., Paramus, New Jersey 07652-4832, or call (201) 265-1248.

Children's Museum at Rockingham
Rockingham Historic Site
Princeton, New Jersey

As part of the Rockingham Historic Site, the Children's Museum makes history come alive for children by surrounding them with an environment typical of 18th-century life. Hands-on activities are offered in the museum (a one-room colonial building) and in the kitchen of the Rockingham mansion. Activities include calligraphy, carding wool, a colonial clothes closet, designing a papyrotamia picture, "Fox and Geese" games, sewing a sampler, experiencing a colonial kitchen, and stuffing a pallet with hay.

Built in the early 1700s by John Harrison, Rockingham was General George Washington's last wartime headquarters. It was here, in 1783, where he wrote his farewell address to the troops. The exhibits and displays in the mansion, the museum, and the kitchen help children to become aware of the rich cultural history and beginnings of the United States. The grounds and exhibits are now under the supervision of the New Jersey Department of Environmental Protection.

Besides the hands-on exploratory displays, the museum also offers annual events on special holidays.

Info in brief: A village museum of interest to all ages, with specific activities in a small children's museum on campus.

George Washington's bedroom in his last headquarters, August to November, 1783, while Congress convened in Princeton.

Hours: Wednesday–Saturday, 10 A.M. to 12 P.M. and 1 P.M. to 4 P.M.; Sunday, 1 P.M. to 4 P.M. School groups by appointment.

Unique exhibits: A specific history hands-on children's museum as one exhibit on a larger campus.

Other sites of interest nearby: The many tourist attractions in New Jersey, including Allaire State Park, Grover Cleveland Birthplace, the Hermitage, Six Flags Great Adventure amusement park, Clementon Lake Park amusement park, Black River & Western Railroad, New Jersey Museum of Transportation and much more.

For further information write to the Rockingham Historic Site, 108 CR 518, RD #4, Princeton, New Jersey 08540, or call (609) 921-8835.

Liberty Science Center
Jersey City, New Jersey

The mission of the Liberty Science Center is to offer informal hands-on and exploratory science and technology experiences in order to "inspire, explain, entertain, engage, involve, challenge, motivate and empower" young minds. Conceived in 1977, the actual building was not begun until 1989. The museum now has a staff of 200 and has had more than one million guests.

The distinctive building offers hundreds of exhibits along with the nation's largest IMAX Dome theater. The exhibits are displayed on three theme floors, with interactive demonstrations, discovery room dialogues and multimedia theater presentations available. "The Invention Floor" features structures, energy and light, images, action and effects. "The Health Floor" encourages self-awareness with exhibits on perception, bodies in motion and making lifestyle choices. "The Environment Floor" emphasizes the atmosphere, marine life, a bug zoo and geology.

Besides its own permanent and rotating displays, the center hosts several national touring exhibitions, offers teacher training, and provides special programs and workshops throughout the year.

Info in brief: Large hands-on science museum for children and their caregivers.

Location: In Liberty State Park, Jersey City, a few minutes from New York City. Liberty State Park houses the Statue of Liberty and Ellis Island.

Hours: Exhibits — Tuesday–Sunday, 9:30 A.M. to 5:30 P.M. Kodak OMNI Theater (IMAX)—10 A.M. to 5 P.M., on the hour. Open most holiday Mondays. Closed Thanksgiving and Christmas Day.

Admissions: Exhibits only — adults, $9.50; students/seniors, $8.50; children (2–12), $6.50. OMNI Theater — adults, $7; students/seniors, $6; children (2–12), $5. Theater —$2. Combo tickets are available. First Wednesday of each month from 1 P.M. to closing is "Wide Open Wednesday" when admission is on a "pay-as-you-wish" basis. Memberships are available. Member of ASTC.

Unique exhibits: LSC's signature exhibit is a 700-pound unfolding geodesic aluminum sphere designed by Chuck Hoberman and on "display" in the four-story atrium.

Other sites of interest nearby: Statue of Liberty, Ellis Island Museum, World Trade Center, Six Flags Great Adventure (Jackson), Coney Island's Astroland (Brooklyn) and the many tourist attractions of both New York and New Jersey.

For further information write to the Liberty Science Center, Liberty State Park, 251 Phillip Street, Jersey City, New Jersey 07305-4699, or call (201) 200-1000. Website: www.lsc.org.

The New Jersey Children's Museum
Paramus, New Jersey

The New Jersey Children's Museum, opened in 1992, is a hands-on museum especially for children under 8 years of age. More than 40 permanent exhibits are housed in the 15,000 sq. ft. converted warehouse. Each exhibit area is designed for specific age groups, from the "Baby Nook" to "Science and Technology" for 1st and 2nd graders.

Daily and weekly activities are regularly scheduled along with special events. The permanent exhibits include a working fire engine, an authentic helicopter, a kids-sized grocery, pizzeria, giant waterplay area, a huge interactive kaleidoscope, a castle, costumes, puppets, frogs, magnets, electricity and more.

Info in brief: A hands-on museum for young children (8 years or younger).

Location: One-half mile south of the Ridgewood Avenue Exit of Route 17 and the Garden State Parkway.

Hours: Weekdays, 9 A.M. to 5 P.M.; Summer weekends, 10 A.M. to 5 P.M.; Winter weekends, 10 A.M. to 6 P.M.

The New Jersey Children's Museum.

Admissions: Under 1, free; others, $7.

For further information write to The New Jersey Children's Museum, 599 Industrial Avenue, Paramus, New Jersey 07652, or call (201) 262-5151.

New Mexico

Explora! Science Center
Albuquerque, New Mexico

For further information contact: Explora! Science Center, 40 First Plaza, Galleria, Suite 68, Albuquerque, New Mexico 87102, phone: (505) 842-6188. Member ASTC

Farmington Museum
Farmington, New Mexico

The City of Farmington oversees the management of the Farmington Museum, one main section of which, the Children's Gallery, is a hands-on museum for children. In the Children's Gallery visitors will find the Shadow Room, the Orchard Street Theater, Mirror Games, The Artist's Nook, a small puppet theater, the Frozen Bubble Box, the Ecosurvival video game STUFFEE, and more. Various temporary and traveling exhibits are also on display throughout the year.

Besides the Children's Gallery, the village-type museum houses historic exhibits from pioneering days, a Natural History gallery and traveling shows. Special classes, workshops and events are also offered.

The historic displays include a replica of a 1930s trading post which includes the Bull Pen, an Office and the Pawn Room, along with a corral area outside.

Info in brief: A village museum with one gallery devoted to hands-on activities for children and their caregivers.

Hours: Tuesday–Friday, noon to 5 P.M.; Saturday, 10 A.M. to 5 P.M.

Admissions: No admissions fee, but donations are appreciated.

Other sites of interest nearby: Aztec Ruins National Monument and Aztec Museum. Within 100 miles are Mesa Verde National Park (116 miles), Anasazi

Heritage Center, Salmon Ruins, Chaco Culture National Historical Park and Durgano, Colorado.

For further information write to the Farmington Museum, 302 N. Orchard, Farmington, New Mexico 87401-6227, or call (505) 599-1174 or 1179.

Santa Fe Children's Museum
Santa Fe, New Mexico

Founded in 1985 by four local educators, the Santa Fe Children's Museum opened in its present location in 1989. It is governed by a 21-member Board of Trustees and maintains a staff of 16 paid employees and 100 volunteers. The building and grounds are leased from the State of New Mexico. The building itself was constructed in the 1930s as a national guard armory. The grounds now house a half-acre horticulture garden.

The 5,000 sq. ft. exhibit area houses both temporary and permanent interactive, hands-on displays for children and their caregivers. Permanent exhibits include a Life Science Area, Technical Climbing Wall and a Toddler Area. Movable or rotating exhibits include "Waterworks," "Bubbles," "Make and Take," "Architectural Building Blocks," "Magnet Table," "Maxi-Rollways," "Zeotropes," "Pin Screen," "Sound Dishes," "Pulley Power," "A Thousand Faces," and more.

Special workshops and events are also offered throughout the year. Some special events have included a monthly "Very Special Arts" day, Museum on Wheels (taken to Children's Hospital of New Mexico), Artists in the Museum, Sunday Science, outreach programs and much more. Contact the museum to find out more about these events.

Info in brief: Interactive, hands-on displays with special programs offered throughout the year.

Location: Just south of the Capitol Building and the Plaza.

Hours: (September–May) Thursday–Saturday, 10 A.M. to 5 P.M.; Sunday, noon to 5 P.M.; (June–August) Wednesday–Saturday, 10 A.M. to 5 P.M.; Sunday, noon to 5 P.M.

Admissions: Under 12, $2; adults, $3. Member Association of Youth Museums.

For further information write to the Santa Fe Children's Museum at 1050 Old Pecos Trail, Santa Fe, New Mexico 87501, or call (505) 989-8359.

The 1837 Hagadorn House Museum
Almond, New York

The Hagadorn House was built around 1837 and has been restored to display furnishings and artifacts from that time period. Of special interest to children is the Children's Room with antique dolls, toys, and more. The "Little Gallery" holds changing exhibits which are often of interest to children — old uniforms, old greeting cards, clothing, and more.

The museum is run on an all-volunteer basis. Besides the museum itself, research materials about the area are available in the Archives Room and can be used by appointment only.

Info in brief: An historic museum more of interest to adults, but with exhibits of interest to children.

Location: On Main Street in Almond, New York, at Exit 33 on Rte. 17.

Hours: Friday, 2 P.M. to 4 P.M. or by appointment.

Admissions: Donations accepted.

Other sites of interest nearby: Alfred University, Letchworth State Park, Strong Museum, Niagara Falls and other tourist attractions in Buffalo and Rochester.

For further information write to the Hagadorn House Museum, Almond Historical Society, 7 N. Main Street, Almond, New York 14804, or call (607) 276-5565.

Brooklyn Children's Museum
Brooklyn, New York

The mission of the Brooklyn Children's Museum is to actively engage children in educational and entertaining experiences through innovation and excellence in its exhibitions, programs and collections usage. The primary target age group is school children. It is the oldest museum in the United States designed specifically for children, founded by the Brooklyn Institute of Arts and Sciences in 1899 as an alternative to existing museums, whose exhibits, it was felt, were too sophisticated for children.

The first facility was located in the Adams Building, a Victorian mansion located in Bedford Park (later renamed Brower Park) in Crown Heights. In

Brooklyn Children's Museum (PHOTOGRAPH: RODNEY K. HURLEY).

1929, the museum moved to the Smith Mansion. After a couple of other moves, the permanent facility was built on the site of the Smith Mansion in Brower Park, and opened in 1977. This 35,000 sq. ft. unique underground structure, designed by the architectural firm of Hardy Holzman Pfeiffer Associates, cost $3.5 million with most of the funds provided by the City of New York.

Today, the world's first children's museum is updating its facilities and exhibits, preparing to usher in the new millennium as an institution offering exhibitions and programs that are relevant to the lives of today's children. A newly renovated facility was reopened in 1996. More than 40 full-time and 20 part-time staff worked with several hundred volunteers to get this new facility up and running.

Info in brief: A mainly hands-on science and humanities museum for children and their caregivers.

Location: Corner of Brooklyn and St. Mark's avenues.

Hours: (Winter) Wednesday–Friday, 2 P.M. to 5 P.M.; Saturday and Sunday, noon to 5 P.M.; open noon to 5 P.M. most school holidays. Call the museum hotline number for summer hours.

Admissions: At the time of this writing, a change in fees was being discussed. Contact the museum hotline number before visiting. Member ASTC.

Unique features: The oldest children's museum in the United States.

Other sites of interest nearby: Children's Museum of the Arts, Children's Museum of Manhattan, Staten Island Children's Museum, Brooklyn Botanic Garden and the many other historic sites in New York.

For further information write to the Brooklyn Children's Museum, 145 Brooklyn Ave., Brooklyn, New York 11213, or call the museum hotline — (718) 735-4400 or 4402. Memberships available.

Cayuga County Agricultural Museum
Auburn, New York

The Cayuga County Agricultural Museum is owned and maintained by Cayuga County and is run strictly by volunteer workers.

This village-type museum displays many farm implements dating from 1830 to 1930, along with antique tractors, sleighs and buggies, a 1900s farm kitchen and herb garden, a village square, general store, blacksmith shop, wood & wheelwright shop, creamery, veterinarian's office, a live colony of honey bees (in summer), and more. Although it is not strictly a children's museum, many of the items on display and the set-up of the museum itself is of interest to children.

Of special interest to all ages are the special events held throughout the year: an antique tractor pull (August), "Old Ways" Day in June, and an old-fashioned Christmas with carolers, barbershop quartets, hot cider, Christmas cookies and horse-drawn sleigh rides.

Info in brief: Village museum.

Location: North tip of Owasco Lake, Auburn, New York.

Hours: Memorial Day–Labor Day. June, Saturday and Sunday, 1 P.M. to 5 P.M.; July and August, Wednesday–Sunday, 1 P.M. to 5 P.M.

Admissions: Free.

Unique exhibits or exhibitions: Large collection of farm implements, many of which were patented out of Cayuga County.

Other sites of interest nearby: The William Seward home (Secretary of State under Abraham Lincoln, famous for his part in the purchase of Alaska), listed on the National Registry of Historic Places.

For further information write to Cayuga County Agricultural Museum, c/o Norman Riley, RD 6, Box 263, Auburn, New York 13021-9806, or call (315) 252-5009 or (315) 253-5611.

Children's Museum of Manhattan
New York, New York

The Children's Museum of Manhattan was founded in 1973 with an aim to engage children and their families in a partnership of learning through the arts, literacy, media and communications, science and the environment, and family learning activities. The targeted audience is families with children from 2 to 10 years of age.

The original site was a basement storefront serving Harlem and the Upper West Side residential neighborhoods of Manhattan, and was called G.A.M.E. (Growth Through Art and Museum Experience). By 1984, the museum took its present name, the staff had grown to 20 full-time and 20 part-time members, and many improvements had been made. Currently, the five floors of hands-on exhibits are enhanced with daily family workshops, performances and special events throughout the year.

Info in brief: A hands-on museum for children and their families.

Location: The Tisch Building between Broadway & Amsterdam.

Hours: Wednesday–Sunday and public school holidays, 10 A.M. to 5 P.M. (Monday and Tuesday are for educational programming.) Special hours are offered during some holidays. Contact the museum for a current schedule.

Admissions: Under 1, free; children and adults, $5; seniors, $2.50. Memberships available.

Other sites of interest nearby: Coney Island's Astroland (Brooklyn), Broadway theaters and many other New York attractions.

For further information write to the Children's Museum of Manhattan, The Tisch Building, 212 W. 83rd St., New York, New York 10024, or call (212) 721-1234. Internet site: www.CMOM.org.

Children's Museum of the Arts
New York, New York

In the heart of SoHo, New York's artist community, the Children's Museum of the Arts is dedicated to helping children develop their full artistic potential through the visual and performing arts.

Interactive arts programs and exhibitions for children ages 18 months through 10 years are offered.

Info in brief: An arts museum with an emphasis on the arts for children.

Location: The SoHo district.

Hours and Admissions: Contact the museum for current schedules.

Unique feature: A museum dedicated strictly to the arts for children.

Other sites of interest nearby: The Brooklyn Children's Museum, the Children's Museum of Manhattan, Staten Island Children's Museum, and other New York City tourist attractions.

For further information write to the Children's Museum of the Arts, 72 Spring St., New York, New York 10012, or call (212) 274-0986.

The Discovery Center of the Southern Tier
Binghamton, New York

Opening in The Discovery Center is just that — an opportunity for children to discover things about themselves and their environment. Many of the interactive displays are permanent exhibits, while rotating exhibits are also offered throughout the year. A hands-on policy is enforced.

Some of the exhibits offered include "Giant Market," "EJ Factory," "Retail Store," "Ecology," "Geology," "The Cody Gallery," "Archaeology," "The Plum Dragon," and more. Special workshops, classes and programs are also offered.

Info in brief: A hands-on children's museum especially for children and their caregivers.

Hours: (School year) Tuesday–Saturday, 10 A.M. to 5 P.M.; Sunday, noon to 5 P.M.; (Summer) Monday–Saturday, 10 A.M. to 5 P.M.; Sunday, noon to 5 P.M. Open special holiday Mondays.

For further information write to The Discovery Center of the Southern Tier, 60 Morgan Rd., Binghamton, New York 13903, or call (607) 773-8661.

Erwin Museum
Painted Post, New York

The museum in Painted Post is closed pending relocation into a railroad depot building which is currently being renovated. Projected re-opening date is 1998, and the tentative new name will be "Depot Museum."

For further information write to Town Manager, Town of Erwin, 117 West Water St., Painted Post, New York 14870, or call (607) 962-7021.

Iroquois Indian Museum
Howes Cave, New York

The Iroquois Indian Museum consists of the adult museum, the Nature Park and the Children's Iroquois Museum. The adult museum emphasizes regional archaeology — combining anthropological research with contemporary interests. The building itself is designed to resemble the longhouse and the powerful symbols of Iroquois culture. Exhibits include the largest collection of contemporary Iroquois art and craftwork, major archaeological collections, a performing arts amphitheater, dancers (outside in the summer), festivals, storytelling, an Iroquois log cabin and garden, and more. Various outreach programs, demonstrations, and programs are offered throughout the year.

The Nature Park is a 45-acre site with an emphasis on the Iroquois view of nature. Interpreters are available and guidelines are provided.

The Children's Iroquois Museum interprets the adult museum and also offers children the opportunities to learn to dance in native traditions, fashion clay into a pot, bead a necklace, make a cornhusk doll, use a spear thrower or use a lacrosse stick. Iroquois educators are available at all times. Special events and Family Days are held at various times. Contact the museum to see what special activities are taking place before your visit.

Info in brief: An educational, interpretive three-part museum with one part specially designated for children's exhibits and activities.

Location: Exit 22 off I-88, follow signs, approximately 2 miles.

Hours: (March–December — except for summer) Tuesday–Saturday, 10 A.M. to 5 P.M.; Sunday, noon to 5 P.M. (Summer hours — July 1–Labor Day weekend) Monday–Saturday, 10 A.M. to 6 P.M.; Sunday, noon to 6 P.M. Closed January and February, Thanksgiving Day, Christmas Eve, Christmas Day, and New Year's Day.

Admissions: Under 7, free; children (7–12), $2.50; students (13–17), $4; adults, $5; seniors, $4.

Unique exhibits: Entire museum dedicated to Iroquois history, traditions and culture.

Other sites of interest nearby: Howe Caverns, Secret Caverns and the old Grist Mill.

For further information write to Iroquois Indian Museum, P.O. Box 7, Caverns Road, Howes Cave, New York 12092, or call (518) 296-8949 or FAX (518) 296-8955.

The Junior Museum
Troy, New York

In existence since 1954, the Junior Museum is currently located at 282 5th Avenue in Troy, New York. Plans call for a move to bigger quarters, however, in the summer of 1998. That location will be 105 8th Street (the Winslow Building).

Both full-time and volunteer workers help to keep current programs running. From its inception, the mission of the museum has been to provide children with hands-on learning experiences in science, history and the arts. Currently, all programs correlate to New York State Elementary Science or Social Studies Curricula and most require advance registration in order to participate, either individually or by classroom. Permanent exhibits are on display, along with changing exhibits in the second floor Art Gallery. The permanent exhibits include a planetarium, Iroquois longhouse, preschool area, "Dolls of the World," habitats exhibits and animal behavior displays. Afterschool programs, a performing arts series, special bus trips, and special scouting programs are also available by advance registration. Outreach programs to local schools are also offered.

Info in brief: Interactive exhibit galleries emphasizing experiences in science, history and the arts for children from preschool ages and up.

Location: The corner of 106th St. and 5th Ave. in downtown Troy. (The museum provides detailed travel instructions to all visitors upon request.)

Hours: Open mostly by reservation, but weekends, Monday mornings and some Fridays are open to the general public. Contact the museum before visiting.

Admissions: Costs vary according to the program chosen, ranging from $2.50 to $20. Be sure to contact the museum. Memberships are available.

Unique exhibits or exhibitions: The planetarium and Iroquois longhouse are of special interest.

Other sites of interest nearby: Mystic Seaport and Aquarium, The Museum of Natural History, CosmoDome and BioDome, and The Bronx Zoo.

For further information write to The Junior Museum, 282 Fifth Avenue, Troy, New York 12182, or call (518) 235-2120.

Lehman College Art Gallery
Bronx, New York

Housed in a building designed by architect Marcel Breuer, the Lehman College Art Gallery caters to young artists, focusing on the encouragement of school-age children to learn about and from the arts. Special programs are available free of charge to members of the community. Programs range from graduate courses for teachers to workshops, after-school and weekend programs for parents and children.

The gallery offers both display exhibits and hands-on art activities.

Info in brief: Art museum with an emphasis on art education for children.

Location: Adjacent to the Jerome Park Reservoir.

Admissions: Free to the public. (Call about special workshops.)

Other sites of interest nearby: Jerome Park Reservoir, Bronx Botanical Gardens and Manhattan tourist attractions.

For further information write to the Lehman College Art Gallery, 250 Bedford Park Boulevard West, Bronx, New York 10468-1589.

Long Island Children's Museum
Garden City, New York

Since its opening in November 1993, the Long Island Children's Museum has emphasized expansion and change. Currently located in space donated by LILCO, the staff and support group hope to eventually become self-supportive and have a permanent location.

Besides special exhibits and group tours, the museum offers five permanent exploration areas. "stART" offers children an opportunity to explore connections as they pull apart and put together pieces of a room-sized sculpture. "Communication Station" offers visitors a chance to explore the various ways people send and receive messages — from the simplest to the newest high-tech methods. "Working on the Railroad" lets children experience life on the railroad. "Bubbles" lets visitors blow bubbles of all shapes and sizes. "What If You Couldn't..." helps children learn about people with disabilities and learn about their own senses.

Info in brief: All exhibits at LICM are interactive, and "hands-on" is the key term used here. All children must be accompanied by an adult. Adults without children must check in at the office.

Location: 550 Stewart Avenue, Garden City, New York 11530.

Gizmo in "stART ROOM" at Long Island Children's Museum.

Hours: Wednesday–Friday, 10 A.M. to 4 P.M.; Saturday and Sunday, 10 A.M. to 5 P.M. Closed Mondays. Open Tuesday for school groups, by appointment. (Call ahead during holiday times.)

Admissions: $4 — general admission; under 2, free. Memberships are available.

Unique exhibits or exhibitions: "stART" emphasizes cooperative learning.

Other sites of interest nearby: Long Island has many tourist attractions, including Old Westbury Gardens, the Cradle of Aviation, the Roosevelt Field shopping mall and miles of beautiful East Coast beaches.

For further information write to the Long Island Children's Museum, 550 Stewart Ave., Garden City, New York 11530, or call (516) 222-0217. Website: http://www.516web.com/MUSEUM/licm.htm.

Long Island Culture History Lab & Museum
Stony Brook, New York

Although more than 10,000 children visit the Long Island Culture History Lab & Museum, it is only open to the public for group tours. Two main programs are offered: Colonial Life & Technology and Long Island Native Life & Archaeology.

Info in brief: A hands-on children's archaeological discovery experience. Open only to groups.

For further information write to the Long Island Culture History Lab & Museum, P.O. Box 1542, Stony Brook, New York 11790, or call (516) 929-8725.

The Marble School House
Eastchester, New York

The Marble School House was built in 1835 and is now open to the public by appointment only. The Eastchester Historical Society provides a "teacher"

The Marble School House.

who will take visitors through a day's activities similar to what students would have experienced at that time.

Info in brief: Historical site which offers a typical 1835s day of schooling experiences.

Hours and Admissions: Open by appointment only. Be sure to contact the museum before visiting.

For further information write to The Marble School House, c/o Eastchester Historical Society, P.O. Box 37, Eastchester, New York 10709, or call (914) 793-1900.

Sci-Tech Center
Watertown, New York

Advertised as "a playground for the mind," the Sci-Tech Center is an interactive science museum with over 40 hands-on exhibits. Also offered are special workshops throughout the year, school tours and special annual events sponsored by the museum.

Many of the exhibits at the museum center around electricity, biology, and light. Other exhibits include a reaction timer, sand pendulum, binary numbers display, magnets, pulleys and more.

Location: Downtown Watertown within walking distance of other attractions.

Hours: Tuesday–Saturday, 10 A.M. to 4 P.M.; also by appointment.

Admissions: Adults, $2; under 18, $1.50; under 3, free; family, $7.50. Memberships available.

Other sites of interest nearby: Jefferson County Historical Museum, historic Downtown Watertown shopping district, two whitewater rafting groups, Thompson Park Zoo, Salmon Run Mall, Watertown Indians (Class A baseball), and the Thousand Islands vacation region. Call the Greater Watertown Chamber of Commerce (315) 788-4400 or Thousand Islands International Council 1-800-8-ISLAND (847-5263).

For further information write to Sci-Tech Center, 154 Stone St., Watertown, New York 13601, or call (315) 788-1340.

Science and Discovery Center
Horseheads, New York

For further information contact: Science and Discovery Center, Arnot Mall, Route 17, Horsehead, New York 14845, phone: (607) 739-5297. Member ASTC.

Sciencenter
Ithaca, New York

Supported by such notables as the late Carl Sagan and Ann Druyan, the mission of the Sciencenter is to offer people of all ages the opportunity "to experience the excitement of scientific exploration and discovery ... through interactive exhibits and programs." The museum started as a hands-on science program at a local elementary school, but became a museum in 1984. After occupying several temporary homes, the museum moved into Phase I of its permanent quarters in 1993. Phase II opened in 1996, and Phase III (a 10,000 sq. ft. addition) is scheduled to begin in 1999.

Currently four full-time and four part-time employees run the museum along with over 250 volunteers. The staff oversees more than 80 hands-on educational exhibits in the museum proper, which includes an outdoor science park. Programs for at-risk youth, school visits, after-school outreach programs and public events are also offered.

The Sciencenter is the only community-built science museum in the world. Other unique features: It is the only outdoor science park in upstate New York, it is the world's only public connection to the National Lightning Detection Network, and it made the world's first Internet connection via local cable TV network.

Info in brief: Over 80 hands-on exhibits especially of interest to children, but appealing to all ages; large museum with innovative exhibits and programs.

Sciencenter.

Location: Corner of First and Franklin streets in upstate Ithaca, New York.

Hours: Tuesday–Saturday, 10 A.M. to 5 P.M.; Sunday, noon to 5 P.M. Open only these Monday holidays — M.L. King, Jr., President's Day, Memorial Day, Labor Day, and Columbus Day.

Admissions: Under 4, free; ages 4–12, $3.50; 13 and over, $4.50; 65 and older, $4.25. Group rates vary. Memberships available. Member ASTC.

Unique exhibits: 17-foot-tall ball machine, Emerson Science Park, and more.

For further information write to Sciencenter, 601 First Street, Ithaca, New York 14850-3507, or call (607) 272-0600 or FAX (607) 277-7469. E-mail: scictr@sciencenter.org. Website: http://www.sciencenter.org.

Scotia-Glenville Children's Museum
Scotia, New York

After fifteen years, the Scotia-Glenville Children's Museum remains a unique traveling museum. The basic mission is to "stimulate curiosity and interest in learning; enrich the school curriculum, and serve children, families, and the general public of all ages." Now chartered by the New York State Board of Regents, the museum services all educational institutions within a 50-mile radius of Scotia, New York, including fairs and festivals, scout troops, libraries, hospitals, nursing homes and retirement centers, and more. Funding comes from various sources — from the Town of Glenville and Village of Scotia, grants and contributions from various foundations, corporations and individuals, as well as from fees for the programs themselves.

Twenty-five part-time museum teachers operate the programs while offices and storage are now located at a permanent site.

Info in brief: Hands-on programs geared to specific groups, but limited to the area in and around Scotia — approximately a 10-county area.

For further information write to Scotia-Glenville Children's Museum, 102 North Ballston Avenue, Scotia, New York 12302, or call (518) 346-1764 or FAX (518) 377-6593.

Sony Wonder Technology Lab
New York, New York

Children of all ages can explore the latest technology on a simplified scale at Sony's Wonder Technology Lab. In the "Environmental Research Studio," kids help out in simulated environmental emergencies. In the "Medical

Imaging Lab," kids learn about technology and modern medical devices. At "Sony Wonder Television Studio," kids can produce their own 6 o'clock news or mix their own 16-track recording at the "Sony Recording Studio." Sony's "Interactive Theater" allows kids to vote on the ending of a movie. A multimedia sculpture, "Gizmo," allows children to take apart and "resculpture" his parts.

Info in brief: An interactive, participatory technology museum for children and their caregivers.

Location: Madison Avenue between 55th and 56th streets.

Hours: Tuesday and Friday, 10 A.M. to 9 P.M.; Wednesday, Thursday and Saturday, 10 A.M. to 6 P.M.; Sunday, noon to 6 P.M.

Admissions: Free.

For further information call the Sony Wonder Technology Lab at (212) 833-8100.

Staten Island Children's Museum
Staten Island, New York

Founded in 1974, the Staten Island Children's Museum is now housed in a three-story building provided by the City of New York. The museum is committed to introducing children to experiences that enrich their knowledge of themselves and the world around them and is continuing to do so by providing award-winning interactive exhibitions in art, science and the humanities.

Exhibits on display in 1996-97 included "Adventures in Three Dimensions" (art and technology), "Wonder Water," "Bugs & Other Insects," "Block Harbor," "WKID" (cameras and the media), "Walk-In! Workshop" (visual arts), "Portia's Playhouse" (theater) and more.

Info in brief: Interactive and hands-on exhibits especially for children and their caregivers.

Location: Snug Harbor Cultural Center.

Hours: Tuesday–Sunday (Summer) 11 A.M. to 5 P.M.; (school year) noon to 5 P.M.

Admissions: Under age 2, free; others, $4.

Unique exhibits: Ten-foot-tall "Praying Mantis" sculpture by the artist Robert Ressler stands at the entrance where children are invited to climb on its wood and steel exoskeleton.

Other sites of interest nearby: New York tourist attractions.

For further information write to the Staten Island Children's Museum, 1000 Richmond Terr., Staten Island, New York 10301-9910, or call (718) 273-2060 (Ext. 147) or FAX (718) 273-2836.

North Carolina

Discovery Place
Science & Technology Museum
Charlotte, North Carolina

The Discovery Place is a large science and technology museum for children and their families. Besides the many hands-on exhibits available, visitors can experience a planetarium show, "Challenger Center," a Rainforest, a Science Circus, Aquarium, Life Center, Omnimax Theater, collection displays, and much more. A new contemporary food court featuring several nationally recognized chain restaurants is now also on campus.

Opened in 1981, Discovery Place has become a major tourist attraction with over 140,000 sq. ft. of major exhibit areas. Many displays are permanent, but there are also rotating and changing exhibits on display throughout the year. Special workshops, educational programs, campouts and other activities are also offered.

Discovery Place.

Info in brief: One of the largest children's museums in the country, emphasizing hands-on displays.

Location: Uptown Charlotte between 6th and 7th streets. Easily accessible from I-77 and I-85. (Suggested parking off the corner of 6th Street and Church Street — $3.)

Hours: Exhibit Hall — (June–August) 9 A.M. to 6 P.M., 7 days a week; (September–May) Monday–Friday, 9 A.M. to 5 P.M.; Saturday and Sunday, 9 A.M. to 6 P.M.; Omnimax/Planetarium — (June–August) Monday–Wednesday, 9 A.M. to 6 P.M.; (September–May) 9 A.M. to 5 P.M.; (year round) Thursday–Saturday, 9 A.M. to 8 P.M.; Sunday, 1 P.M. to 8 P.M.

Admissions: General admissions plus one option — under 3, free; ages 3–5, $2.75; seniors (60+), $4.50; youth (6–12), $4.50; others (13–59), $5.50. Each additional option is $2. Memberships with special options are available. Member ASTC.

Other sites of interest nearby: Nature Museum, Paramount's Carowinds amusement park, Santa's Land amusement park, and Tweetsie Railroad (Blowing Rock).

For further information write to Discovery Place, 301 N. Tryon St., Charlotte, North Carolina 28202, or call (704) 372-6261 or 1-800-935-0553.

Imagination Station
Wilson, North Carolina

For further information contact: Imagination Station, 224 E. Nash Street, P.O. Box 2127, Wilson, North Carolina 27893, phone: (919) 291-5113. Member ASTC.

Nature Museum
Charlotte, North Carolina

Touching, encountering and discovering nature has been the main emphasis at the Nature Museum since it opened in 1946. Programs on wildlife, hands-on exhibits, a puppet theatre, live creatures and a scenic nature trail make this a top educational resource both to school groups and the general public. A new addition is "Grandpa Tree," star of the new "Creatures of the Night" exhibit. Grandpa is an animated storytelling tree who helps visitors learn about nature and science.

Info in brief: A hands-on nature center where children are encouraged to touch and participate.

Nature Museum.

Location: Southeast Charlotte, adjacent to Freedom Park.

Hours: Monday–Friday, 9 A.M. to 5 P.M.; Saturday, 10 A.M. to 5 P.M.; Sunday, 1 P.M. to 5 P.M. Closed Thanksgiving, Christmas Eve and Day, New Year's and Easter.

Admissions: Under 3, free; others, $2.

Unique exhibits: Grandpa Tree.

Other sites of interest nearby: Discovery Place, Paramount's Carowinds amusement park, Santa's Land amusement park, and Tweetsie Railroad (Blowing Rock).

For further information write to Nature Museum, 1658 Sterling Road, Charlotte, North Carolina 28209, or call (704) 337-6261 or 337-2660.

The Rocky Mount Children's Museum
Rocky Mount, North Carolina

The Rocky Mount Children's Museum is a division of the City of Rocky Mount Parks and Recreation Department. It is a hands-on museum with exhibits on science, technology and history. Main exhibit areas include: "The News Zone," a multimedia recreation of a television broadcast news experience; "Kidspace," an interactive play area for children 6 years and younger; "The Civitan Planetarium"; "The Living Marsh," a 600-gallon saltwater touch pool; "Animal Gallery"; "The Edison Effect," an historical exhibit chronicling Thomas Alva Edison's life; and "Indians of the Tar River," an historical diorama of the culture of the Tuscarroa Indians. Various temporary exhibits are also offered about three times each year.

Info in brief: Hands-on museum for young children and their caregivers.

Hours: Monday–Friday, 10 A.M. to 5 P.M.; Saturday, noon to 5 P.M.; Sunday, 2 P.M. to 5 P.M.

Admissions: Under 3, free; children (4–15), $1; adults, $2; seniors (60+), $1. Wonderful Wednesday offers free admission from 2 P.M. to 5 P.M. Memberships available. Member ASTC.

Other sites of interest nearby: Ten other children's museums located in North Carolina: National Railroad Museum in Hamlet, Great Smoky Mountains Railway in Dillsboro, North Carolina Transportation Museum in Spencer, Wilmington Railroad Museum in Wilmington, Ghost Town in the Sky in Maggie Valley, Paramount's Carowinds amusement park in Charlotte, Santa's Land in Cherokee, and Tweetsie Railroad amusement park in Blowing Rock.

For further information write to The Rocky Mount Children's Museum, 1611 Gay Street, Rocky Mount, North Carolina 27804, or call (919) 972-1167 or FAX (919) 972-1232.

SciWorks
Winston-Salem, North Carolina

SciWorks offers visitors more than 45,000 sq. ft. of hands-on exhibits, along with a 15-acre environmental park, a 120-seat state-of-the-art planetarium, demonstrations, special programs and special events. All exhibits and programs are based on science and the environment.

SciWorks first opened in 1965 as the Nature Science Center, with an emphasis on the environment. Expansions and improvements have added the hands-on science experiments and the planetarium to the list of opportunities for visitors to explore.

Info in brief: A hands-on museum and nature center especially for children and their caregivers, but of interest to all age groups.

Location: Off U.S. Hwy. 52 on Hanes Mill Road.

Hours: Monday–Saturday, 10 A.M. to 5 P.M.; Sunday, 1 P.M. to 5 P.M. Extended hours and free admission on 2nd Friday of each month (to 8 P.M.). Park facilities close at 4:30 P.M.

Admissions: (General admissions) under 3, free; children (3–5) $2; youth and seniors, $4.50; adults, $6. (Planetarium) under 3, free; all others, $2. Combination tickets available. Member ASTC.

For further information write to SciWorks, 400 Hanes Mill Road, Winston-Salem, North Carolina 27105, or call (910) 767-6730.

North Dakota

The Children's Museum at Yunker Farm
Fargo, North Dakota

Yunker Farm Park is owned and maintained by the Fargo Park Board. The Children's Museum, started in 1985, is housed in a historic building leased from the Park Board. The original part of the building was built in 1876 as a farmhouse. Additions have increased the floorspace to 4000 sq. ft., enabling the museum to house over 50 hands-on educational exhibits.

Outside, visitors can ride a train and a carousel. A playground and picnic area are also available. Special programs offered include outreach classes for local schools, Yunkie Club for preschoolers and "Think Thursday."

Info in brief: Hands-on museum for children 12 and under and their families.

Hours: Monday, Tuesday, Wednesday, Friday, and Saturday, 10 A.M. to 5 P.M.; Thursday, 1 P.M. to 8 P.M.; Sunday, 1 P.M. to 5 P.M.

Admissions: Under 1, free; others, $3; Thursday—Dollar Day. Train and carousel tickets are extra. All children must be accompanied by an adult. Member of Association of Youth Museums.

Unique exhibits: Train and carousel outside.

For further information write to The Children's Museum at Yunker Farm, 1201 28th Ave. N., Fargo, North Dakota 58102, or call (701) 232-6102.

Gateway to Science Center
Bismarck, North Dakota

For further information contact: Gateway to Science Center, 2700 State Street, Gateway Mall, Bismarck, North Dakota 58501, phone: (701) 258-1975. Member ASTC.

Ohio

Children's Museum of Cincinnati
Cincinnati, Ohio

Officially opened in 1994, the Children's Museum of Cincinnati features seven major exhibit areas with over 200 hands-on experiences for children 12 and under and their families. Live performances, special programs, workshops and outreach programs are also offered. The seven major areas are "Sounds Around — Good Vibration" (physics of sound), "Jungle Moves — Walk on the Wild Side" (body experiences), "Media Dimensions" (videotaping and theatrics), "Shapes Relate" (create and measure geometric patterns), "The Works" (tools and machines), "Where in the World Are You?" (culture and travel), and "Kids Cover, Baby, Beach, Toddler Tidepool" (early learning area).

The 30,000 sq. ft. building (25,500 sq. ft. dedicated to exhibits) is part of the revitalization plan for downtown Cincinnati. Many restaurants and other museums are close by.

Info in brief: A hands-on children's museum with over 200 experiences for pre-adolescents and younger children.

Location: In historic Longworth Hall, downtown Cincinnati.

Hours: Wednesday, Thursday, and Sunday, noon to 5 P.M.; Friday, noon to 8 P.M.; Saturday, 10 A.M. to 5 P.M. Summer and school holiday hours are somewhat longer. Open Tuesday during summer.

Admissions: Children 5 and younger pay their age in dollars. All other visitors pay $6. Member AYM.

Other sites of interest nearby: Americana amusement park (Middletown), Fantasy Farm amusement park (Middletown), Paramount's Kings Island, I&O Scenic Railway, and other Cincinnati tourist attractions.

Cincinnati Fire Museum
Cincinnati, Ohio

Along with other fire museums across the country, the Cincinnati Fire Museum showcases the history of fire fighting in the area from the early 1800s to the present. This fire museum, however, does more than display old equipment, it provides hands-on, participatory exhibits for children. Starting with a video about fire safety, children move on into the museum to explore an old water pumper fire truck, slide down a fire pole, call 911, and use three interactive computer programs to learn more about fire safety. Old equipment is on display, along with memorabilia from firefighters through the generations in Cincinnati.

Info in brief: Both hands-on and visual displays are offered.

Location: Downtown Cincinnati in a National Register firehouse at the corners of Court and Plum streets.

Hours: Tuesday–Friday, 10 A.M. to 4 P.M.; Saturday and Sunday, noon to 4 P.M.; closed Monday and holidays.

The Cincinnati Fire Museum is housed in a restored 1907 National Register fire house.

Admissions: Children, $2; adults, $3; seniors, $2.50.

Other sites of interest nearby: BB Riverboats, Inc., Behringer-Crawford Museum, Children's Museum of Cincinnati, Cincinnati Historical Society Museum, Cincinnati Museum of Natural History, Cincinnati Railway Museum, Paramount's Kings Island amusement park, and more.

For further information write to Cincinnati Fire Museum, 315 W. Court St., Cincinnati, Ohio 45202, or call (513) 621-5553.

Cleveland Children's Museum
Cleveland, Ohio

This small museum features four interactive exhibit areas which encourage creative and dramatic play. Intended to serve children ages 2 to 10 years, these areas are: "Over and Under Bridges," "Water-Go-Round," "Little House Under Construction" (rotating exhibit), and at least one other traveling exhibit from the Youth Museum Exhibit Collaborative (YMEC) at all times. The intent is to keep the museum growing and changing.

Info in brief: Hands-on, exploratory museum for children and caregivers.

Location: In the heart of Cleveland's University Circle at the intersection of Euclid Ave. and Martin Luther King Blvd.

Hours: (School year) Tuesday–Friday, 1 P.M. to 5 P.M.; Saturday, 10 A.M. to 5 P.M.; Sunday, noon to 5 P.M.; second Wednesday of each month (Wonderful Wednesday) open to 8 P.M. Summer and holiday hours vary. Contact the museum before visiting.

Admissions: Under age 2 and seniors, free; ages 2 to 15, $4; 16 and older, $5. Memberships available. Member ASTC.

Other sites of interest nearby: Cleveland Orchestra, Cleveland Museum of Art, Cleveland Museum of Natural History, African American Museum, the Cleveland Playhouse, Cleveland Clinic, Western Reserve Historical Society, the Health Museum.

For further information write to the Cleveland Children's Museum, 10730 Euclid Ave., Cleveland, Ohio 44106-2200, or call (216) 791-7114 or FAX (216) 791-8838.

COSI
Center of Science & Industry
Columbus, Ohio

For further information contact: COSI, Center of Science & Industry, 280 E. Broad St., Columbus, Ohio 43215-3773, phone: (614) 228-2674. Member ASTC.

McKinley Museum
Canton, Ohio

Originally founded in 1946, the McKinley Museum is actually a combination of several interrelated museums sitting on a 26-acre area. On the museum grounds is the double-domed granite National Memorial (and burial place) of President William McKinley, the McKinley Museum of History, Science & Industry and the Planetarium. The Museum of History, Science & Industry includes several areas itself — the McKinley Gallery, Ramsay (Presidential) Research Library, Historical Hall, Everhard Auditorium, Ralph Wilson Memorial Garden and, most important for this book, "Discover World." Many collections on exhibit include the largest collection of McKinley memorabilia in the world, a 300-item doll collection, an antique toy and train collection and miniature train layout, an 1840–1940 costume exhibit, a valentine and post card exhibit and more.

Discover World is of special interest to children. Exhibits are both visual and exploratory. As visitors enter the area, they are greeted by the roar of a life-sized, robotic Allosaurus. Dioramas of early lifestyles fill this area. A series of ponds filled with real plant and animal life invite you to use inverted periscopes to see what is happening underwater. A working beehive is also on display here. Near the end of the visit is Space Station Earth — a scientific laboratory with hands-on exhibits for children to explore. To round out the tour, a visit to the Planetarium finishes the experience from past, to present and then into the future — space.

Over 200 people, both full-time employees and volunteers, work at the museum throughout the year. Most exhibits are permanent, but various educational programs are offered along with cooperative community activities.

Info in brief: Definitely a full-day experience with both hands-on and visual displays available.

Location: 800 McKinley Monument Drive N.W., Canton, Ohio (It is suggested that you send for the brochure which has specific travel instructions.)

Hours: Monday–Saturday, 9 A.M. to 5 P.M.; Sunday, noon to 5 P.M. (Open until 6 P.M. during the summer.)

Admissions: Adults, $6; ages 3–18, $4; seniors (60 and over), $5. Member ASTC.

Unique exhibits or exhibitions: Many — send for the brochure.

Other sites of interest nearby: Tourist attractions in Cleveland, Ohio, or Pittsburgh, Pennsylvania.

For further information write to the McKinley Museum, 800 McKinley Monument Dr. N.W., Canton, Ohio 44708-4800, or call (216) 455-7043 or FAX 330-455-1137.

Oklahoma

Omniplex
Oklahoma City, Oklahoma

The Omniplex contains three independent museums in one 10-acre facility. However, visitors pay only one admissions charge, which covers all three museum areas. Museums included are the Kirkpatrick Science and Air Space Museum, the International Photography Hall of Fame and Museum, and Red Earth Indian Center. Of special concern to this publication is the Kirkpatrick Science and Air Space Museum, which itself contains five main areas. These

One of the many hands-on activities available at Omniplex.

areas are the Hands-on Science Museum, the Air Space Museum, Kirkpatrick Galleries, Botanical Gardens and Greenhouse, and Kirkpatrick Planetarium.

The Hands-on Science Museum has been operating for nearly 40 years. Its primary aim is and has always been to promote science literacy in Oklahoma. Today, it is considered to be the premier interactive science center in Oklahoma, with over 300 hands-on exhibits and numerous educational programs. Some of the theme exhibit areas include: Perception, Light, Sound, Life Sciences, Energy Sources, Meteorology, KIDSPACE, Physics, Agriculture and Nutrition. In 1996, *Parents* magazine named the Hands-on Science Museum as one of the nation's best museums for children.

The Air Space Museum was founded in 1980 to "recognize and honor those in aviation and space who have contributed significantly to the advancement of aviation and space exploration." (Oklahoma has produced more astronauts than any other state.) One-week summer camp programs offer an extensive aerospace experience for children ages 3–16. Visitors can experience a NASA moon landing, fly an actual mission at the AWAC's control center, fly a real WWII link trainer, fly an F-16 Combat Flight Simulator, and man a unique Mercury capsule simulator that recreates the first space mission by a U.S. astronaut.

The other areas of the Kirkpatrick Science and Air Space Museum are also of interest to children and their families, but offer little in the way of hands-on experiences. Displays of miniatures, toys, and wildlife, however, are enough to hold their interest, so plan on allotting an entire day to this visit.

Info in brief: A multifacility museum with plenty of hands-on activities and interactive displays for children of all ages and their caregivers. Also includes a planetarium, botanical gardens and more.

Location: In northeast Oklahoma City near the zoo and Remington Park racetrack.

Hours: (Memorial Day–Labor Day) Monday–Saturday, 9 A.M. to 6 P.M.; Sunday, 11 A.M. to 6 P.M. (Day after Labor Day–day before Memorial Day) Monday–Friday, 9 A.M. to 5 P.M.; Saturday, 9 A.M. to 6 P.M.; Sunday, 11 A.M. to 6 P.M. Closed Thanksgiving and Christmas Day. Planetarium show times vary, so be sure to contact museum for updated schedule.

Admissions: Under 2, free; children (3–12), $4; adults, $6.50; seniors (65+), $4.50. Member ASTC.

Unique feature: Seven museums under one roof.

Other sites of interest nearby: Oklahoma State Firefighters Museum, Amateur Softball Association, National Softball Hall of Fame and Museum, Lions Family Fun Park, The National Cowboy Hall of Fame and Western Heritage Center, Oklahoma City Zoo, Remington Park (horse racing), and Frontier City theme park.

For further information write to Omniplex, 2100 N.E. 52nd St., Oklahoma City, Oklahoma 73111-7198, or call 1-800-LEARN KC or (405) 424-5545 or FAX (405) 424-5106.

Will Rogers Memorial & Birthplace
Claremore, Oklahoma

The Will Rogers museum in Claremore is an eight-gallery comprehensive museum with three theaters, two interactive television kiosks and the

Will Rogers Museum (note Rogers' tomb in foreground).

family tomb. The museum also features a 3,000 sq. ft. children's participation area (opened in 1995). Children enter a time tunnel that starts with the Oklahoma mound dwellers of 20,000 years ago. The tunnel takes them past exhibits of the exiled 19th-century Cherokee Indians' civilization, past exhibits of taxi-dermed indigenous wildlife, past live fish and live red ants, then ends in the hands-on area depicting Will Rogers' career. Many role-playing situations are available here.

Info in brief: There are actually two attractions situated about 12 miles apart, one of which (in Claremore) offers participatory activities for children.

Location: The museum is in Claremore; the Living History Ranch is on the shore of Lake Oologah.

Hours: Daily, 8 A.M to 5 P.M.

Admissions: Under 12, $3; adults, $4; seniors, $3. Contact the museum for current charges.

Unique feature: The only museum in the world dedicated to maintaining the memory and humor of Will Rogers.

For further information write to the Will Rogers Memorial & Birthplace, P.O. Box 157, Claremore, Oklahoma 74018-0157, or call 1-800-324-WILL or (918) 341-0719 or FAX (918) 341-8246. Website: http//www.willrogers.org.

Oregon

The Children's Museum
Southern Oregon Historical Society
Jacksonville, Oregon

The Southern Oregon Historical Society operates several museums and historical sites that are open to the public. One of these museums is The Children's Museum in Jacksonville. Opened in 1979, the museum is located in the 1910 former Jackson County Jail. Exhibits target children aged from preschool through fourth grade. It is a history museum which provides hands-on history for all ages. The two floors of exhibits include an actual 1890s General Store, a Chinese laundry, a bank, and several other stations that encourage interactive play. The newest exhibit is titled "Miner, Baker, Furniture Maker"—chronicling technology's role in the development of early Jacksonville and Southern Oregon.

Info in brief: The Children's Museum is a hands-on, interactive museum for young children and their caregivers. Other museums run by the society are of interest to the whole family.

Location: 206 N. 5th Street, Jacksonville.

Hours: (Summer — Memorial Day–Labor Day) daily, 10 A.M. to 5 P.M. (Winter) Wednesday–Saturday, 10 A.M. to 5 P.M.; Sunday, noon to 5 P.M.

Admissions: Under 6, free; children (6–12), $2; adults, $3; seniors (55+), $2.

Other sites of interest nearby: (Operated by the society) The Southern Oregon History Center, Jacksonville Museum of Southern Oregon History, the C.C. Beekman House, and more; Enchanted Forest amusement park in Turner; Oaks Park in Portland; The Gilbert House Children's Museum in Salem; and the Oregon Museum of Science and Industry in Portland.

For further information write to The Children's Museum, 206 N. 5th St., Jacksonville, Oregon 97530, or c/o Southern Oregon Historical Society, 106 N. Central Ave., Medford, Oregon 97501-5926, or call (541) 773-6536 or FAX (541) 776-7994.

The Gilbert House Children's Museum
Salem, Oregon

Opened in 1989, the Gilbert House Children's Museum is a hands-on museum whose mission is "to provide innovative and stimulating experiences to spark children's natural creativity and curiosity ... with fun and challenging exhibits and activities in the Sciences, Arts and Humanities." Each room and each exhibit has written guides, educational explanations, and lesson concepts posted for a more thorough understanding of each activity.

The museum grounds incorporate two two-story buildings which house various exhibits, including: "Recycle City," "Wet & Wild," "Artist Studio," "Cave of Wonders," "Secret Sleuths," "Kidspace," "Gilbert Room" (memorabilia display), "Chain Reaction" (physics), "Bienvenidos a México!," "Karaoke for Kids," "Children's Theater," a family resource center, classroom space, and various rotating exhibits throughout the year. Use of the portable planetarium is available at various times and visitors are also allowed access to the Children's Discovery Garden.

Info in brief: Mostly hands-on museum designed for children.

Location: Housed in two historic Victorian homes on Salem's downtown riverfront.

Hours: Tuesday–Saturday, 10 A.M. to 5 P.M.; Sunday, noon to 4 P.M.; open Monday March through June only. Closed most major holidays.

Admissions: Under 1, free; seniors, $3 and after 3:30 P.M.; all others, $4. Member of Association of Youth Museums. Member ASTC.

Other sites of interest nearby: Elsinore Center for the Arts, Enchanted Forest (in Turner, 7 miles south), Oaks Park amusement park (Portland).

For further information write to The Gilbert House Children's Museum, Inc., 116 Marion Street NE, Salem, Oregon 97301-3437, or call (503) 371-3631. Website: http://www.teleport.com/-explore or explore@teleport.com.

The High Desert Museum
Bend, Oregon

The cultural and natural heritage of the "Intermountain West" is brought to life at the High Desert Museum. Situated on a 150-acre tract of land surrounded by the Deschutes National Forest, the museum offers visitors unusual activities both outside and inside. Outside, the rugged land between the Rockies and the Cascades, a unique area of timberland, rivers, volcanic hot springs and high desert land, enables the museum to offer visitors opportunities to observe otters in a pond, witness hand-feeding of native porcupines, watch a birds of prey presentation, walk through a settler's cabin and hike the trails. Inside, visual displays, hands-on activities, and interactive displays enable visitors to rediscover the sights and sounds of the past.

Info in brief: An indoor-outdoor museum offering a number of hands-on activities along with visual and interactive displays for the whole family.

Location: Six miles south of Bend, Oregon.

Hours: Open every day, 9 A.M. to 5 P.M. Closed Thanksgiving, Christmas and New Year's Day. Be sure to contact the museum for exact times of various demonstrations throughout the day.

Admissions: Small fee charged. Memberships available.

Other sites of interest nearby: Deschutes National Forest, numerous outdoor recreational facilities. Contact the Chamber of Commerce and Tourist Bureau in Bend, Oregon, for more specific details.

For further information write to The High Desert Museum, 59800 South Highway 97, Bend, Oregon 97702, or call (503) 382-4754.

Oregon City Carnegie Center for Kids
Carnegie Children's Center
Oregon City, Oregon

The Carnegie Center was built in 1913 as a public library — one of the many public libraries built with funds donated by steel millionaire Andrew Carnegie. The building contains 17-foot ceilings with vertical grain fir beams.

Now known as the Carnegie Center, the building currently houses an Arts Center, Coffee Shop and the Children's Center and is operated under the direction of Oregon City Parks and Recreation.

The Children's Center is a hands-on children's museum featuring a pint-sized grocery store, credit union, hospital, soda fountain, fire engine, an amphibian display and more.

Info in brief: The Children's Center is a strictly hands-on museum, but the entire building would be of interest to the whole family.

Location: Historic Carnegie Library building, which sits on a one-acre park.

Hours: Monday–Friday, 9 A.M. to 7 P.M.; Saturday, 10 A.M. to 6 P.M.; Sunday, 1 P.M. to 5 P.M.

Admissions: $2 per child. (All children must be accompanied by an adult.) Member of the "Children's Museums Across the Pacific Northwest" (see Appendix).

Other sites of interest nearby: Children's Museum in Portland, Gilbert House Children's Museum in Salem, Southern Oregon Historical Society Children's Museum in Jacksonville, Umpqua Discovery Center in Reedsport, Children's Museum of Eastern Oregon in Pendleton, Oh! Zone Children's Museum in Joseph, Wonder Works in The Dalles, and Williamette Science & Technology Center (WISTEC) in Eugene.

For further information write to the Oregon City Carnegie Center, Children's Center, 606 John Adams St., Oregon City, Oregon 97405, or call (503) 557-9199.

Oregon Museum of Science and Industry
Portland, Oregon

Founded in 1944, OMSI started, as many children's museums do, in a house. After an unprecedented fundraising campaign, the huge new facility opened in 1992 on Water Avenue. Six exhibit halls, including seven interactive laboratories and an Early Childhood Education Center, a 330-seat Omnimax Theater, a 220-seat Murdock Sky Theater Planetarium/Laser Light Venue, the USS *Blueback* (a 219 ft. diesel electric submarine), a Science Store, Cafe and a 25,000 sq. ft. exhibit shop are offered. A total of 219,000 sq. ft. are incorporated in the facility. The five permanent exhibit halls represent specific scientific themes: Earth Science, Life Science, Information Science, Physical Science and Space Science. All halls house laboratories and hands-on activity areas as well as live science presentations throughout the day.

Besides the in-house exhibits and programs, the museum offers 26 traveling exhibits to museums throughout North America, making it the largest science outreach program in the United States.

Info in brief: A hands-on, participatory science museum for children and their caregivers.

Location: S.E. Water Ave. at the East end of the Hawthorne Bridge on the Willamette River.

Hours: (Winter, March 1–May 23) Friday–Wednesday, 9:30 A.M. to 5:30 P.M.; Thursday, 9:30 A.M. to 8 P.M. (Summer, May 24–September 1) Friday–Wednesday, 9:30 A.M. to 7 P.M.; Thursday, 9:30 A.M. to 8 P.M.

Admissions (Prices shown are for adults, then seniors and youth): Museum (including planetarium show)—$9.50, $8. Omnimax Theater—$4.50, $4. Submarine—$3.50, $3.50. All four attractions—$15.50, $13.50. Laser light shows—matinee, $2; evening, $6.50. Memberships available.

Unique exhibits: The facility incorporates the Historic Portland General Electric Turbine Hall, which once generated power for downtown Portland.

For further information write to OMSI, 1945 SE Water Ave., Portland, Oregon 97214-3354, or call (503) 797-4000. Website: http://www.omsi.edu.

Pacific Northwest Museum of Natural History
Ashland, Oregon

Opened in July of 1994, the Pacific Northwest Museum of Natural History includes exhibits and dioramas depicting habitats of the Pacific Northwest in its 30,000 sq. ft. building (15,600 sq. ft. of actual museum space). These exhibits are bound together by an interactive computer system which encourages visitors to better understand the hows and whys of nature. "Please DO Touch" signs are in evidence throughout the discovery center which is oriented toward children and includes live animals and plants with interactive activities. Live animal programs are offered year round along with permanent and traveling exhibits.

The museum claims to be at the forefront of the new museums that are concept-based rather than collections-based. It offers multisensory natural exhibits, interactive video adventures, and hands-on games and experiments to encourage a better understanding of scientific principles and ecosystems.

Info in brief: A nature center which emphasizes hands-on activities for children and their caregivers.

Location: 15 miles north of the California-Oregon border between the Siskiyou and Cascade Mountain ranges.

Hours: (May–December) 10 A.M. to 4 P.M., daily; (January–April) Wednesday–Sunday, 10 A.M. to 4 P.M.

Admissions: Under 3, free; children (5–15), $4.50; seniors (62+), $5.50; adults (16–61), $6.50. Member ASTC.

Other sites of interest nearby: Crater Lake National Park, the Oregon Shakespeare Festival, the Peter Britt Music Festival, Cascade Lakes Tour, and Oregon Caves National Monument.

For further information write to the Pacific Northwest Museum of Natural History, 1500 East Main St., Ashland, Oregon 97520, or call (541) 488-1084 or FAX (541) 482-1115.

(Portland) Children's Museum
Portland, Oregon

Celebrating more than 45 years of service, the Children's Museum in Portland is now administered by the Portland Bureau of Parks and Recreation.

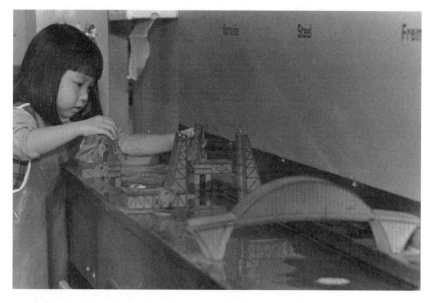

One of the unique exhibits found in the Portland Children's Museum (PHOTOGRAPH: *JULIE KEEFE*).

Little visitors (especially those ages infant to 10 years) are encouraged to use their imaginations as they slip into a firefighter's gear, climb onto a ladder truck, rev up pint-sized vehicles and follow roadways through a tunnel and bridge, pretend to operate a repair shop, restaurant, doctor's office, grocery store and more. The basement houses a clay workshop where all visitors may play with the clay for free, or can purchase their completed creations for a small fee. A playground is also located just outside in Lair Hill Park.

In conjunction with the museum — and just a short distance away — is the Children's Cultural Center, where contemporary American Indian life is explored. A 1,200 sq. ft. exhibit called "Living Legends" opened early in 1997, along with other cultural exhibits.

Admission to the Children's Museum includes free admission to the Cultural Center, or each museum may be visited separately.

Info in brief: A hands-on museum for younger children with some exhibits of interest to slightly older children. The Cultural Center attracts visitors of all ages.

Locations: In older downtown Portland.

Hours: Every day, 9 A.M. to 5 P.M. Closed some national holidays.

Admissions: Under 1, free; $3.50 for others. Member AYM.

Unique exhibits: "H$_2$Oh" exhibit — pumps, drawbridges and a bubble wall impel visitors to experiment.

Other sites of interest nearby: Cascade Sternwheelers, Crooked River Railroad Company Dinner Train, End of the Oregon Trail Interpretive Center, The High Desert Museum, Metro Washington Park Zoo, Mount Hood Railroad, Oregon Museum of Science and Industry, and more.

For further information write to the Children's Museum, 3037 SW Second Ave., Portland, Oregon 97201, or call (503) 823-2227 or FAX (503) 823-3667.

Southern Oregon Historical Society Children's Museum
Jacksonville, Oregon

The Southern Oregon Children's Museum has two main themes or "timelines" showing historic events in Oregon history from the 1850s to the 1930s. One timeline shows domestic events while the other emphasizes occupational changes. All hands-on activities in these areas offer children a chance to handle reproductions of objects from the past.

The 23 exhibits include an 1890s General Store, a Takeima Indian Lodge, a schoolroom, an 1890s kitchen, a pioneer cabin, a pioneer bank and a laundry.

Special family-type activities are also offered seasonally: Spring — Public Heritage Fair; Summer — Ice Cream Social; Winter — Victorian Christmas; and Fall — Multicultural Heritage Day. It is recommended to contact the museum before planning a visit.

Info in brief: Hands-on activities along with interpretive displays make this museum of interest to the whole family, with specific items just for children.

Hours: (Memorial Day to Labor Day) open daily, 10 A.M. to 5 P.M.; (Labor Day to Memorial Day) Tuesday and Sunday, noon to 5 P.M. and Wednesday–Saturday, 10 A.M. to 5 P.M.

Admissions: Age 5 and under, free; ages 6 to 12, $2; 12 and over, $3.

Unique exhibitions: All exhibits based on Oregon history.

Other sites of interest nearby: Oregon Shakespeare Festival in Ashland, South Oregon History Center in Medford, the Beekman House (Living History) in Jacksonville and the Natural History Museum in Ashland.

For further information write to the Southern Oregon Historical Society Children's Museum, 106 N. Central Ave., Medford, Oregon 97501-5926, or call (541) 773-6536 or FAX (541) 776-7994.

Umpqua Discovery Center
Reedsport, Oregon

The Umpqua Discovery Center is dedicated to two themes displayed in two exhibit wings — the "Umpqua Experience Wing" and the "Antarctic Experience Wing." In the Umpqua Experience Wing, visitors learn how the water, land and people shaped and changed each other. The "Landscape" exhibit offers a "hands-on" computerized topographic display, and the "Oceans, Beaches, Dunes and Forests" exhibit teaches visitors about the geology of the area, through interactive displays and a do-it-yourself working weather station.

Umpqua Discovery Center.

The Antarctic Experience Wing teaches about the role the United States played in the exploration of the Antarctic. Displays include a guided tour of the *HERO*, a wooden sailing ship especially built for scientific exploration of the Antarctic, memorabilia, equipment and even a "bigger than life" statue of Admiral Richard Byrd.

The building also includes a theater with a wide variety of video tapes available, a 35-foot periscope and accessibility to the Boardwalk along the Umpqua River waterfront.

Info in brief: A unique nature center with some hands-on activities for children.

Location: On the scenic Umpqua Riverfront in Reedsport.

Hours: (Summer — June 1–September 30) daily, 9 A.M. to 5 P.M. (Winter — October 1–May 31) daily, 10 A.M. to 4 P.M. Closed Thanksgiving, Christmas, and New Year's Day.

Admissions: Under 5, free; children (5–12), $1.50; adults, $3.

Unique exhibits: Antarctic display and oceanside experiences.

Other sites of interest nearby: Many Reedsport–Winchester Bay area tourist attractions such as the Boardwalk, Jet Boats, Oldtown, Oregon Dunes National Recreation Headquarters, Umpqua River Lighthouse and Umpqua beaches.

For further information write to the Umpqua Discovery Center, 409 Riverfront Way, Reedsport, Oregon 97467, or call (541) 271-4816. E-mail: discover@mail.coos.or.us.

WISTEC
(Williamette Science & Technology Center)
Eugene, Oregon

Established in 1961, WISTEC is a science and technology center whose primary focus is to provide hands-on activities for children of all ages. Three or four major rotating exhibits are on display each year, including national touring exhibits and exhibits built by WISTEC personnel.

Also offered are exhibit-related activities, special classes, summer camps, outreach programs and group tours.

Info in brief: Hands-on children's museum.

Location: Across from Autzen Stadium.

Hours: Hours vary with different programs. Contact the museum before visiting.

Admissions: Member of the "Children's Museums Across the Pacific Northwest" (see Appendix).

Other sites of interest nearby: See Oregon City Carnegie Center for Kids.

For further information write to WISTEC, 2300 Leo Harris Parkway, Eugene, Oregon 97401, or call (541) 687-3619 or FAX (541) 484-9027. E-mail: wistec@efn.org.

Pennsylvania

Briar Bush Nature Center
Abington, Pennsylvania

This 12-acre woodland and wildlife sanctuary opened in 1962 as an educational facility, after having been an exclusive refuge since 1908. The site now offers both indoor activities in "The Center" and outdoor facilities to enhance the visitor's learning experience.

The center offers hands-on exhibits and games, natural history displays, live animals, a "Discovery Den," a crawl-through cave exhibit for guided

Live animals are one of the many attractions of Briar Bush Nature Center.

groups, a library, gift shop, and kitchen facilities. The outdoors area offers diverse habitats and woodchipped trails, a pond, a bird observatory, wildflower garden, active beehive, three-tier deck and wildlife.

Numerous special programs and workshops are offered, along with ecological trips and more.

Info in brief: Hands-on nature experiences and experiments for children and their caregivers.

Hours: Trails open dawn to dusk. The center, pond and observatory are open 9 A.M. to 5 P.M., Monday–Saturday; Sunday, 1 P.M. to 5 P.M.

Admissions: Free. Some charges for some special programs.

Unique exhibits: Children are actually encouraged to handle nature, not just look at it.

For further information write to Briar Bush Nature Center, 1212 Edgehill Road, Abington, Pennsylvania 19001, or call (215) 887-6603.

Childventure Museum and Shop
Fort Washington, Pennsylvania

Childventure is a hands-on museum specifically for children 1 to 10 years of age. Interactive play spaces, cultural exhibits and imaginative play areas are offered along with state-of-the-art video programs. Changing exhibits are

One of the imaginative play areas in Childventure Museum and Shop.

offered in the main exhibit area frequently, and occasionally in one of the smaller areas.

Info in brief: Hands-on participatory and some visual exhibits especially for children and their caregivers.

Location: Fort Washington Office Park.

Hours: Tuesday–Saturday, 10 A.M. to 4 P.M.; Sunday, 12 P.M. to 4 P.M. Closed Mondays except Columbus, Martin Luther King, Presidents' and Memorial Days. Also closed Thanksgiving, Christmas, New Year's Day, July 4th and the last two weeks of August.

Admissions: Children, $5; adults, $4.

For further information write to Childventure, 430 Virginia Dr., Fort Washington, Pennsylvania 19034, or call (215) 643-3233.

Hands-on House
Lancaster, Pennsylvania

Located in an historic Victorian farmhouse, Hands-on House features eight self-directed interactive exhibit areas geared for children ages 2 to 10 years. Discovery areas include "Space Voyage Checkpoint," "Once Upon a Forest," "Under Construction," "The Whatchama-Giggle Company," "Face to Face," "Corner Grocery," "Eye Spy," and "Switch on Art."

Besides the self-directed areas, the museum also offers special classes, workshops, special scout workshops, and group tours.

Info in brief: Hands-on, interactive exhibits for ages 2 to 10.

Location: In the heart of Lancaster County, just north of Lancaster, close to Routes 30 and 272.

Hours: Memorial Day to Labor Day — Monday–Thursday and Saturday, 10 A.M. to 5 P.M.; Friday, 10 A.M. to 8 P.M.; Sunday, 12 P.M. to 5 P.M. Labor Day to Memorial Day — Closed Monday; Tuesday–Thursday, 11 A.M. to 4 P.M.; Friday, 11 A.M. to 8 P.M.; Saturday, 10 A.M. to 5 P.M.; Sunday, 12 P.M. to 5 P.M. Group visits by reservation at other times also.

Admissions: $4 (subject to change without notice). Memberships available.

Other sites of interest nearby: Lancaster County tourist attractions.

For further information write to Hands-on House, Children's Museum of Lancaster, 2380 Kissel Hill Road, Lancaster, Pennsylvania 17601, or call (717) 569-KIDS (5437).

Peter J. McGovern Little League Museum
Williamsport, Pennsylvania

The Little League Museum is the only sports museum dedicated to a child's game, and consequently would be of interest to children. Although it is not a strictly hands-on museum, the eight theme rooms each offer some interactive participation for visitors. These themes are: the Lobby (with one of the largest photographic murals in the world), the Founders Room, the Play It Safe Room, the Play Ball Room (where visitors can bat and throw in safety cages), the Showcase Room, the Hall of Excellence, the Gallery of Achievement, and the Theater.

Now in its eleventh year of operation, the museum showcases the development of Little League from its inception in 1939 as a three-team league to its current 2.5 million membership standing. The museum is full of displays, pictures, videos, and exhibits showcasing players, equipment, rules, history, the future and the fun of Little League.

Info in brief: A concept-based museum with interactive displays of specific interest to children and their families, especially those interested in sports. Some hands-on activities, but mostly interactive, computer-controlled exhibits.

Location: On U.S. Route 14, adjacent to the Little League Baseball World Series Stadium and the Little League International Headquarters.

Hours: Monday–Saturday, 9 A.M. to 5 P.M.; Sunday, noon to 5 P.M. After Memorial Day, closing time is 7 P.M. Closed Thanksgiving, Christmas and New Year's Day.

Admissions: Under 5, free; children (5–13), $1.50; seniors, $3; Other adults, $5. Family rate, $13. Member of AAM.

For further information write to the Peter J. McGovern Little League Museum, P.O. Box 3485, Williamsport, Pennsylvania 17701, or call (717) 326-3607.

Pittsburgh Children's Museum
Pittsburgh, Pennsylvania

The Pittsburgh Children's Museum is located in the historic Old Post Office Building, Allegheny Center, on Pittsburgh's North Side. Since its beginning in 1983, its mission has been "to enrich the lives of children" through the use of exhibits, artifacts, performances, interactive demonstrations, art activities and more. The goal is to foster creativity, discovery, learning and understanding.

The three-story building offers loads of hands-on fun through the use of permanent and revolving interactive exhibits, as well as visits by children's book authors and illustrators, Mister Rogers' Neighborhood puppets, Jim Henson puppets, Andy Warhol prints, "Stuffee" (a nine-foot-tall, blue-haired health exhibit), art activities in The Workshop, a recreation of a life-like street environment which teaches bicycle, school bus, car and pedestrian safety, and much more.

The museum also has a tremendous outreach program which includes assemblies, classroom programs, hands-on workshops, traveling trunks, festival arts packages and teacher classes for certification. Special classes and workshops are also offered throughout the year.

Info in brief: Three floors of hands-on exploratory exhibits — both permanent and revolving — for all ages.

Location: 10 Children's Way, Allegheny Center, Pittsburgh, Pennsylvania.

Hours: Tuesday–Saturday, 10 A.M. to 5 P.M.; Sunday, noon to 5 P.M.; open till 8 P.M. one Thursday per month (call 322-5058, press 6); Monday, open for groups.

Admissions: $4 per person; under 2, free; $2 on Thursday. Member ASTC.

Unique exhibits or exhibitions: "Stuffee" (the museum's trademark) — a nine-foot tall, blue-haired anatomy exhibit which unzips to reveal his internal organs (in pillow form) to illustrate how our bodies work. "Safety Street," a recreation of a life-like street environment to teach safety rules.

Other sites of interest nearby (phone numbers given): Carnegie Science Center (237-3400), Frick Art & Historical Center (371-0600), Carnegie Museums of Pittsburgh (622-3131), Duquesne Incline, The Andy Warhol Museum (237-8300), Tour-Ed Mine & Museum (224-4720), Riverboat Cruises (355-7980), and much more. Call the Visitor Information Hotline at 1-800-366-0093 for more information.

For further information write to The Pittsburgh Children's Museum, 10 Children's Way, Pittsburgh, Pennsylvania 15212-5250, or call (412) 322-5058 (recorded info.) or (412) 322-5059 (bus. office). E-mail: pcm@pop,usaor.net.

Please Touch Museum
Philadelphia, Pennsylvania

The Please Touch Museum is probably the only museum in the country designed for children ages 7 or younger. All exhibits encourage children to touch, ride, climb, or otherwise interact with the materials provided.

For further information write to The Please Touch Museum, 210 N. 21st St., Philadelphia, Pennsylvania 19103, or call (215) 963-0667. Member ASTC.

Puerto Rico

Museo del Niño
San Juan, Puerto Rico

One little-known tourist attraction in San Juan is the Museo del Niño, a hands-on museum for children. Exhibits on display include "Pueblito" (play-space for kids 1–3 years old), "Gozando con Numeros" (math exhibit), "Diseno con Texturas" (creating designs with textures), "Dibuyo en Espajos" (drawing on mirrors), "La Barberia" (barber shop), "Vistitemos al Dentista," "Camerino" (imaginative play), "La Placita" (kids play in a traditional Puerto Rican town square), "Hazlo con Reciclaje" (art with recyclables), "Carpinteria" (using tools and wood), "Amigos de Aquí y Alla" (shortwave radio station — Saturdays only), "Nuestro Ambiente" (experience the ecosystems of Puerto Rican Rain Forests), "Burbujas" (soap bubbles and solar lighting), "Mi Mascota y Yo" (pet ownership), "Aedes Agypti" (microscopes and mosquitos), and "Observatorio" (using a powerful telescope to view solar spots).

Museo del Niño.

Special activities and events are also offered at various times throughout the year. Contact the museum before visiting for a current schedule of events.

Info in brief: A small hands-on museum for children and their caregivers.

Location: Historic Old San Juan, Puerto Rico, next to the Convento Hotel on Cristo Street.

Hours: Tuesday–Thursday, 9 A.M. to 3 P.M.; Friday, 10 A.M. to 5 P.M.; Saturday and Sunday, 12:30 P.M. to 5 P.M.

Admissions: All visitors, $2.

Other sites of interest nearby: All of Old San Juan is a historical monument. Visitors can see Spanish architecture, El Morro Fortress, several museums, and the governor's mansion. Shopping and restaurants are also major tourist attractions.

For further information write to Museo del Niño, P.O. Box 9022467, San Juan, Puerto Rico 00902-2467 (no extra postage is required), or call (787) 722-3791 or (787) 725-7214 or FAX (787) 723-2058.

Rhode Island

The Children's Museum of Rhode Island
Pawtucket, Rhode Island

At the time of this writing the Children's Museum of Rhode Island was undergoing major changes, including moving to a new facility, a name change, and all-new exhibits. Plans are to have definite plans completed by 1998. For further information, call (401) 726-2591 or (454) 4759.

South Dakota

Discovery Center & Aquarium
Pierre, South Dakota

The Discovery Center opened in 1989 and is the only Sci-Tech Center in South Dakota that is open year-round. The museum currently offers more than 60 hands-on exhibits for children. Most exhibits are geared around

Discovery Center & Aquarium (Pierre, South Dakota).

science explorations, especially in electricity and magnetism. Three aquariums with fish from the Missouri River are also on display, and planetarium shows are offered regularly. A permanent observatory and a Children's Science Theater are planned to open soon.

Info in brief: A hands-on, participatory science museum for children of all ages and their caregivers.

Hours: (Winter) Sunday–Friday, 1 P.M. to 5 P.M.; Saturday, 10 A.M. to 5 P.M.; (Summer) Monday–Saturday, 10 A.M. to 5 P.M.; Sunday, 1 P.M. to 5 P.M.

Admissions: Under 3, free; children (3–12), $1.75; adults, $3. Member ASTC.

Other sites of interest nearby: Historic Fort Chouteau, Verendrye Museum, South Dakota National Guard Museum, the State Capitol, Fighting Stallions Memorial, Capitol Grounds Arboretum Trail, and the South Dakota Cultural Heritage Center.

For further information write to the Discovery Center & Aquarium, 805 West Sious Avenue, Pierre, South Dakota 57501, or call (605) 224-8295 or FAX (605) 224-2865. Website: sddcaklm@sd.cybernex.net.

Tennessee

Boone Cabin Children's Museum
Netherland Inn Boat Yard Complex
Kingsport, Tennessee

The Boone Cabin Children's Museum is part of the historic complex called the Netherland Inn Boat Yard Complex, which is listed on the National Register of Historic Places. The inn itself is a three-story stone and frame structure with a two-story detached back wing. First a King's Boat Yard boarding house in 1802, it was also a stagecoach inn, and, later, a famous inn and tavern. During its inn days, famous visitors included Andrew Jackson, Andrew Johnson and James K. Polk. Among the several outbuildings is the Boone Cabin Children's Museum.

The two-room cabin that houses the children's museum is a small log structure which once was the Duffield, Virginia, home of Daniel Boone and his family. This fine example of early pioneer construction has been faithfully preserved and currently sits on the site of a Netherland Inn's slave cabin.

The cabin provides a hands-on experience with books, old and handmade toys, games and period furnishings. Children and guests are encouraged to touch the furnishings and even visit the loft.

Info in brief: A village museum with this small unique hands-on children's history museum. Many special events are also held on the grounds at various times during the year.

Location: On the bank of the Holston River in the historic Boatyard District.

Hours: (May–October) guided tours, Saturday and Sunday, 2 P.M. to 4:30 P.M. Group tours available at other times.

Admissions: Under 6, free; students, $1; seniors, $2; adults, $3. Memberships available.

Other sites of interest nearby: Allandale Mansion, Appalachian Caverns, Bays Mountain Park & Planetarium, Exchange Place (farm complex), Fort Patrick Henry Dam, Warriors' Path State Park.

For further information write to Netherland Inn Boat Yard Complex, 2144 Netherland Inn Road, Kingsport, Tennessee 37660, or call (615) 247-3211.

The Children's Museum of Memphis
Memphis, Tennessee

Opened in 1990, The Children's Museum of Memphis aims to provide interactive exhibits and programs in the arts, sciences, humanities and technology for children ages 12 or younger.

The museum now occupies more than 50,000 sq. ft. of floor space in four buildings which formerly housed the National Guard. The main exhibit area, called CitySpace, covers 12,000 sq. ft. and is a child-sized city with a bank,

CityFriends Exhibit at The Children's Museum of Memphis.

city services area, skyscraper, garage, grocery store, toddler play area, dentist offices, clock tower, recycling center, and a changing exhibits gallery where major new hands-on exhibits are made available to the visitor several times throughout the year.

Info in brief: Hands-on museum for children ages 12 or younger.

Hours: Tuesday–Saturday, 9 A.M. to 5 P.M.; Sunday, noon to 5 P.M.; closed Monday and some holidays.

Admissions: Under 1, free; children (1–12), $4; adults (13–61), $5; seniors (62+), $4. Member ASTC.

Other sites of interest nearby: Liberty Bowl Memorial Stadium, Mid-South Fairgrounds, Memphis Zoo, Pink Palace Museum, and other Memphis attractions.

For further information write to The Children's Museum of Memphis, 2525 Central Ave., Memphis, Tennessee 38104, or call (901) 458-2678 or FAX (901) 458-4033.

Hands On! Regional Museum
Johnson City, Tennessee

The mission of the Hands On! Regional Museum is to create a dynamic, educational, fun environment which stimulates discovery, thought and

Hands On! Regional Museum.

understanding through interactive exhibits, programs and events in the arts, sciences and humanities. After a feasibility study in 1985-86, Phase I of the museum opened in 1986. After several more "phases" and transitions, the museum eventually underwent two facility renovations, several upgradings of exhibits, a name change and several changes in leadership to become a 15,000 sq. ft., active children's museum.

Besides the permanent displays, the museum offers daily programs, weekend programs, a special monthly "club" workshop, outreach programs and more.

Info in brief: A hands-on, interactive museum for children and their caregivers.

Hours: Monday (June–August only), 9 A.M. to 5 P.M.; Tuesday–Friday, 9 A.M. to 5 P.M.; Saturday, 10 A.M. to 5 P.M.; Sunday, 1 P.M. to 5 P.M.

Admissions: Under 3, free; ages 3 and 4, $3; all others, $4. Memberships available. Children under 13 must be accompanied by an adult. Member ASTC.

Other sites of interest nearby: Dollywood and Pigeon Forge (Pigeon Forge), Opryland U.S.A. (Nashville), and Libertyland Theme Park (Memphis).

For further information write to Hands On! Regional Museum, 315 E. Main St., Johnson City, Tennessee 37601, or call (423) 434-HAND. Website: http://www.thewebcorp.com/handson/handson.htm.

Hands-On Science Center
Tullahoma, Tennessee

For further information contact: Hands-On Science Center, P.O. Box 1121, 101 Mitchell Blvd., Tullahoma, Tennessee 37388, phone: (615) 455-8387. Member ASTC.

The Museum of East Tennessee History
Knoxville, Tennessee

Since opening its doors in 1993, the Museum of East Tennessee History has been committed to interpreting 200 years of that region's history. The museum, operated by the East Tennessee Historical Society, offers both permanent and changing exhibits. The permanent exhibit contains interactive components and audio segments to attract visitors. True to its mission, the museum is housed in the historic U.S. Custom House and Post Office, built in 1874.

Info in brief: A history museum with some interactive activities for children.

Location: Next to Krutch Park in the East Tennessee Historical Center (Old Custom House) at Market Street and Clinch Avenue in downtown Knoxville.

Hours: Tuesday–Saturday, 10 A.M. to 4 P.M.; Sunday, 1 P.M. to 5 P.M.

Admissions: Under 6, free; students, $2; adults, $3; seniors, $2.50.

Other sites of interest nearby: Market Square, the "Old City" and other Tennessee tourist attractions.

For further information write to the Museum of East Tennessee History, 600 Market St., Knoxville, Tennessee 37902, or call (615) 544-4318.

Texas

Austin Children's Museum
Austin, Texas

The Austin Children's Museum is a private, nonprofit hands-on museum which offers both permanent and changing exhibits. Monthly calendars update visitors to the ever-changing special events and workshops sponsored by the museum. The museum also sponsors an International Children's Festival each year.

Info in brief: Hands-on participatory museum for children of all ages and their families.

Hours: Tuesday–Saturday, 10 A.M. to 5 P.M.; Sunday, noon to 5 P.M.

Admissions: $2.50 general admission. Free admission for children under age 2; for all visitors on Sunday from 4 P.M. to 5 P.M. and Wednesday from 5 P.M. to 8 P.M. An "open door policy" provides free admission to all who ask. Member ASTC.

Other sites of interest nearby: Tourist attractions in Austin.

For further information write to the Austin Children's Museum, 1501 W. 5th St., Austin, Texas 78703, or call (512) 472-2499. Website: http://www.amplify.com/ACM.

Children's Discovery Center
Rusk County History Museum
Depot Museum Complex
Henderson, Texas

The Depot Museum Complex houses the Rusk County History Museum and the Children's Discovery Center. Also situated on the 4-acre site are eight other restored buildings from the area's past. The complex includes an 1841 log cabin, an early 1900s printing shop, country doctor's office, reconstructed barn, broom shop, the famous Arnold Outhouse (see below), the Beall-Ross home, a red caboose and a syrup mill. A former 1901 Missouri-Pacific Depot houses the waiting rooms and station master's office and the cotton warehouse which has been converted into the children's learning center. All nine buildings combine to make an interesting village museum, of which one area is a children's exploratory museum.

Info in brief: Village museum with one small area dedicated to hands-on, exploratory experiences for children.

Hours: Monday–Friday, 9 A.M. to 5 P.M.; Saturday, 9 A.M. to 1 P.M. (closed noon to 1 P.M.); Genealogy Center open 1 P.M. to 5 P.M. weekdays. Closed on all state and federal holidays.

Admissions: Children, $1; adults, $2.

Unique exhibits: The Arnold Outhouse is the most publicized historical marker in Texas. It consists of a three-holer outhouse with louvered windows and a porch.

For further information write to the Depot Museum Complex, 514 N. High St., Henderson, Texas 75652, or call (903) 657-4303.

The Children's Museum in New Braunfels
New Braunfels, Texas

The Children's Museum in New Braunfels is a hands-on, exploratory museum for children of all ages. Some of the exhibits offered include "Where in the World?," "Once Upon a Time," "CMN-TV," "Magic School Bus Science Corner," "Puppet Place," "Picnic in the Park," "Grandma's Attic," and "Make 'N' Take" (recyclable arts center). Workshops, classes, and special events are also offered.

Info in brief: A small hands-on museum especially for younger children and their caregivers.

Location: New Braunfels Factory Stores, Suite 530. Exit 188 off IH-35 (new location).

Hours: Monday–Saturday, 9 A.M. to 5 P.M.; Sunday, 10 A.M. to 5 P.M.

Admissions: Under 1, free; all others, $2.50. Memberships available.

Other sites of interest nearby: Rio Raft Co. rafting tours, the New Braunfels Conservation Society living history museum buildings and the other shops in the New Braunfels Factory Stores mall.

For further information write to The Children's Museum in New Braunfels, 651 Business Loop I-35 N, Suite 530, New Braunfels, Texas 78130, or call (210) 620-0939.

The Children's Museum of Houston
Houston, Texas

The Children's Museum of Houston uses multilingual and nonverbal information in its displays, encouraging children of all ages and abilities to experience the displays without the stress of having to read instructions. The museum opened in 1992 with 11 permanent exhibits and two changing exhibit galleries, and a philosophy of providing "enjoyable, participatory and educational exhibits for children, families, and teachers." Even though the targeted ages for children is 6 months to 12 years, exhibits are designed to interest accompanying adults and people of different reading abilities.

Permanent exhibit areas include "Beginnings" (visual history of the museum), "Kid-TV," "How Does It Work" (phones, automobiles, and other technology), "The Tot Spot" (for preschoolers), "New Perspectives Gallery" (two cultural exhibitions about Mexico and Taiwan), "Farm to Market," "Expressions" (open art studio), "Our Small Planet" (environment), "Experimentations" (open science lab), and "The Magic School Bus Inside the Earth."

Info in brief: A hands-on museum for children and their caregivers.

Location: In Houston's museum district —1500 Binz at the Corner of Binz and LaBranch.

Hours: Tuesday–Saturday, 9 A.M. to 5 P.M.; Thursday, until 8 P.M.; Sunday, noon to 5 P.M.

Admissions: Under 2, free; all others $5 until 3 P.M.; after 3 P.M., $3. Member ASTC.

Other sites of interest nearby: Several museums within walking distance, Southern Orient Express DRC Rail Tours, Texas Limited train excursion,

AstroWorld amusement park, WaterWorld water park, and other Houston tourist attractions.

For further information write to The Children's Museum of Houston, 1500 Binz, Houston, Texas 77004-7112, or call (713) 522-1138 or FAX (713) 524-6471 or 522-5747.

Discovery Place
Texarkana, Texas

The Texarkana Museums System actually consists of three museums in downtown Texarkana. The Ace of Clubs House (ca. 1880–1940), the Texarkana Historical Museum, and the Discovery Place. The Discovery Place is the only building which would really qualify as a children's museum. Several hands-on exhibits help children learn about the past with such displays as the Caddo people's grass hut, an old school house, and a real early–Texas cooking kitchen. Children and their families can also learn about some basic scientific principles through exhibits that teach about speed and the power of momentum, and more.

Info in brief: A hands-on and historical museum for children and their caregivers. Part of a tri-plex of museums which would interest the whole family.

Location: Downtown Texarkana at 3rd and Pine streets.

Hours: Tuesday–Saturday, 10 A.M. to 4 P.M.

Admissions: Prices vary with package chosen. Write or FAX for detailed information.

For further information write to the Discovery Place, c/o Texarkana Museums System, P.O. Box 2343, Texarkana, Texas 75504-2343, or call (903) 793-4831 or FAX (903) 793-7108.

Houston Fire Museum, Inc.
Houston, Texas

The Houston Fire Museum is located just south of Downtown Houston in historic Fire Station No. 7. Its mission is to educate the public about the importance of fire and life safety and to teach the history of fire service. Visitors can view exhibits showing the evolution of firefighting from the days of the "bucket brigades" to today's advanced firefighting and lifesaving services.

Several pieces of antique fire apparatus are housed there, including a 1938 Rex Reo truck (open for children to explore), an old steam engine and a 1912 water tower. Other displays include collections of smaller pieces of equipment, patches, gear, and more.

The building itself is listed on the National Register of Historic Places. When first opened in 1899, it housed horse-drawn equipment, a steam engine and a hose wagon. It was one of Houston's busiest fire houses for many years. After being closed for 12 years, it was renovated and reopened in 1982 as the museum and is now open both for individual visitors and group tours.

Info in brief: The exciting nature of the exhibits makes it of special interest to children. The only true hands-on exhibit is the 1938 Rex Reo firetruck with firefighting gear on board for children to wear as they fight imaginary fires with the equipment also on board. Group tours are not recommended for children under 5 years of age.

Location: 2403 Milan Street, Houston, Texas.

Hours: 10 A.M. to 4 P.M., Tuesday–Saturday. (Other times also available for special group tours.)

Admissions: "Nominal"—call for more information.

Unique exhibits or exhibitions: 1938 Rex Reo firetruck and firefighting equipment and gear.

Other sites of interest nearby: The many tourist attractions of Houston.

For further information write to the Houston Fire Museum, 2403 Milam Street, Houston, Texas 77006, or call (713) 524-2526, or FAX (713) 520-7566.

Laredo Children's Museum
Laredo, Texas

This small children's museum is located in an old military building on the campus of Laredo Community College. Hands-on exhibits include "Grocery Store," "Computer Room," "Construction Corner," "Pediatric Clinic," "Choo-Choo Train," "Stage & Theatre," and "Sound Pipes." Traveling exhibits are made available to visitors several times a year. Super Sunday Programs, summer camps, and weekend workshops and special festivals are also offered.

Info in brief: A small hands-on arts and humanities museum for young children and their caregivers. Near the Mexican border, this would make a nice side-trip after an exhausting Mexico-shopping trip.

Location: On the campus of Laredo Community College, right on the Rio Grande.

Hours: Wednesday–Sunday, 1 P.M. to 5 P.M.; Saturday, 10 A.M. to 5 P.M.

Admissions: Children, $1; adults, $2.

Other sites of interest nearby: Mexican-American border.

For further information write to the Laredo Children's Museum, West End Washington St., Laredo, Texas 78040, or call (210) 725-2299 or FAX (210) 725-7776.

Museum of the Southwest
Midland, Texas

The Museum of the Southwest was founded in 1965 by the Junior League of Midland to honor the ancestral heritage of those who forged the new life in the Great Southwest. An art museum was the first step in this plan to preserve the history, art and culture of the area. The museum complex has grown to include the Turner Mansion with art galleries (Thomas Gallery and the South Wing Exhibition Hall), the Marian Blakemore Planetarium (added in 1972), and the Fredda Turner Durham Children's Museum (begun in 1986).

The Children's Museum sits on property neighboring the Turner Mansion and offers a number of science and art exhibitions. Both permanent and rotating exhibits are available to the visitor. Some exhibits include The Lowe Learning Center (computer lab with software programs in Science, Strategy/ Thinking Skills, Art/Music/Creativity, and Read-Along Books; Imagination Station (dress-up, role-playing area); Light and Color; and more. Six-day art courses are also offered for the young artist, along with special weekend workshops, summer concerts and more.

The Blakemore Planetarium offers a variety of programs throughout the year. Visitors should call ahead for updated schedules and to insure seating through the reservations clerk.

The museum was accredited by the American Association of Museums in June of 1992.

Info in brief: A complex of three museums, all of which are of interest to children, but one of which is specifically a hands-on museum for children.

Location: In Midland, midway between El Paso and Dallas on I-20.

Hours: Tuesday–Saturday, 10 A.M. to 5 P.M.; Sunday, 2 P.M. to 5 P.M. Planetarium showtimes differ slightly. Contact the Planetarium before your visit.

Admissions: Free, to the Art Museum and the Fredda Turner Durham Children's Museum.

Other sites of interest nearby: The American Airpower Heritage Museum, and the Petroleum Museum.

For further information write to the Museum of the Southwest, 1705 W. Missouri Ave., Midland, Texas 79701-6516, or call (915) 683-2882 or (915) 570-7770 or FAX (915) 570-7077.

The National Center for
Children's Illustrated Literature
Abilene, Texas

The NCCIL was established after a group of people became concerned about children and the arts, specifically literature. This group wanted to create a place where the best of the worlds of libraries, museums, art and education could be brought together for children and their families. Using exhibits and programming for original illustrations from recently published children's books, the center's aim is to enhance and promote literacy for children.

Located in the old Grace Hotel (a mission-style building originally built in 1909 and renovated in 1992), the Grace Cultural Center now houses the Museums of Abilene and the NCCIL. The museums of Abilene have held the top priority at the center, but current plans are to dedicate approximately 3,000 sq. ft. on the third floor of the building to the NCCIL. Although the first exhibition was held in December 1995, the NCCIL probably will not be in full swing until 1998. This museum/library/education center will feature "The Permanent William Joyce Gallery," "The Main Gallery" (four new shows per year are planned), an orientation/theater, a library/reading room, an activity area with some hands-on and some docent-guided exhibits, and an office. Storytelling, illustration exhibitions, and festivals are among the main activities planned.

Info in brief: More of a visual display/performance-type of museum, but with items of interest specifically for children.

Location: In the Downtown Historic District, across from the restored Texas & Pacific depot.

Hours and Admissions: Not yet established at the time of this writing.

Unique exhibits: The entire concept of a museum with these characteristics as its main interest is a unique concept.

Other sites of interest nearby: Texas & Pacific depot (restored), Museums of Abilene (see listing), and other tourist attractions in Abilene.

Science Land/Denton's Discovery Museum
Denton, Texas

For further information contact: Science Land/Denton's Discovery Museum, 1516 East Windsor, Denton,Texas 76201, phone: (817) 383-8686. Member ASTC.

The Science Place
Southwest Museum of Science & Technology
Dallas, Texas

For further information contact: The Science Place, c/o Southwest Museum of Science & Technology, 1318 Second Ave., Fair Park, P.O. Box 151469, Dallas, Texas 75315-1469, phone: (214) 428-7200. Member ASTC.

Science Spectrum
Lubbock, Texas

The Science Spectrum is a hands-on science and technology center offering exciting demonstrations, interactive hands-on exhibits and exploratory areas. Some of the experiences available include Bubble Fun, "Flight and Space," computer experiences, Kidspace for preschoolers, Whisper Dish and more. Traveling exhibits are offered through the year. Science Saturdays programs are offered free of charge each Saturday. An Omnimax Theater is also on site.

Info in brief: A hands-on children's museum.

Hours: Monday–Friday, 10 A.M. to 5:30 P.M.; Saturday, 10 A.M. to 7 P.M.; Sunday, 1 P.M. to 5:30 P.M.

Admissions: (Museum only) under 3, free; children (3–16), $4.50; adults, $5.50; seniors (60+), $4.50. (Omnimax Theater only) under 3, free; children, $4.75; adults, $5.75; seniors, $4.75. (Combination — both facilities) under 3, free; children, $7; adults, $9; seniors, $7. Member ASTC.

Other sites of interest nearby: Lubbock Lake Landmark State Historical Park, Moody Planetarium of the Museum of Texas Tech, The Museum of Texas Tech University, and Ranching Heritage Center.

For further information write to Science Spectrum, 2579 S. Loop 289, Ste., 250, Lubbock, Texas 79423, or call (806) 745-2525.

Utah

The Children's Museum of Utah
Salt Lake City, Utah

The Children's Museum of Utah (TCMU) was founded in 1978. Doors were opened on the museum, housed in the former Wasatch Warm Springs Plunge building, in 1983. The hands-on exhibits focus on the physical and social sciences, the arts, and world cultures. More than 25 permanent exhibits, a visiting exhibit program, outreach and social service programs, and other interactive programs occupy approximately 19,000 sq. ft. of building space.

There are currently six full-time and three part-time members on the museum's staff. Several volunteers help the staff keep the museum running.

Info in brief: A hands-on museum for children and their caregivers.

Location: Downtown Salt Lake City.

Hours: Monday–Thursday and Saturday, 9:30 A.M. to 5 P.M.; Friday, 9:30 A.M. to 9 P.M. Closed Sundays.

Admissions: Under 2, free; all others, $3.

Unique exhibits: A 747 Flight Simulator.

Other sites of interest nearby: Golden Spike National Historic Site in Brigham City; Heber Valley Railroad in Heber City; Lagoon, Lagoon A Beach, and Pioneer Village in Farmington.

For further information write to The Children's Museum of Utah, 840 North 300 West, Salt Lake City, Utah 84103-1413, or call (801) 328-3383.

Vermont

Montshire Museum of Science
Norwich, Vermont

The name Montshire comes from the combination of Vermont and New Hampshire, which is the area that the museum serves. Opening in 1976 in Hanover, New Hampshire, the museum moved to its larger facility in Norwich, Vermont in 1989. Montshire received the 1996 National Award for Museum Service in 1995, enabling it to receive some grants and monetary awards which will further increase both the size and the quality of the services offered.

Montshire, although not strictly classified as a children's museum, is a hands-on museum with exhibits on natural and physical science, ecology and technology. Outside, more than 110 acres of woodland offer more than 2½ miles of nature trails to explore. Inside, two floors are packed with dozens of hands-on exhibits targeted for visitors of all age ranges. "Explainers" are on hand to answer questions, or visitors are free to explore the facilities on their own. A few special events are held during the year, and school field trips are encouraged. Traveling outreach programs are also offered.

Some major exhibits offered include "A.D.A.M." (Animated Dissection of Anatomy for Medicine — computer program), "Air Flow," "Andy's Place" (for preschoolers), "Bikevator" (energy), "Bubbles," "Dinosaurs Alive" (temporary display), "Electricity Bench" (circuits, resistors, etc.), "Flow Tunnel," "Honeybees," "Kinetic Energy Machine," "Microscopes," "The Lighthouse" (outside), "Mathematics" and much more.

Info in brief: While not advertised strictly as a children's museum, there are plenty of hands-on activities (most exhibits are) in this small museum to keep children (and adults) of all age ranges busy and entertained.

Location: On the banks of the Connecticut River in Norwich, just across the river from Hanover. Exit 13 off I-91 to Montshire Road.

Montshire Museum of Science (© JOHN GILBERT FOX; ALL RIGHTS RESERVED).

Hours: Daily, 10 A.M. to 5 P.M.

Admissions: Under 3, free; children (3–17), $4; adults, $5. Memberships available. Member of ASTC.

Unique feature: Montshire received a $1.2 million National Science Foundation grant to be the lead organization of TEAMS (Traveling Exhibits at Museums of Science), a collaboration of five small science centers, with original exhibits to be shared among the participants.

Other sites of interest nearby: Winter skiing, beaches, Conway Scenic Railroad (North Conway, New York), Hobo Railroad (Lincoln, New Hampshire), The Mt. Washington Cog Railway (Mt. Washington, New Hampshire), White Mountain Central Railroad (Lincoln, New Hampshire), Green Mountain Flyer (Bellows Falls, Vermont), Lamoille Valley Railroad (Morrisville, Vermont), Shelburne Museum (37 historic buildings near Shelburne, Vermont), Alpine Slide at Mount Mansfield Resort (Vermont), Pico Alpine Slide (Rutland, Vermont), Santa's Land amusement park (Putney, Vermont), and five amusement parks in New Hampshire: Canobie Lake Park (Salem), Santa's Village (Jefferson), Six Gun City (Jefferson), Storyland (Glen), and Whale's Tale Water Park (Lincoln).

For further information write to Montshire Museum of Science, P.O. Box 770, Norwich, Vermont 05055, or call (802) 649-2200. Website: http://www.valley,net/~mms/.

Virginia

Chesapeake Planetarium
Chesapeake, Virginia

Although not strictly a children's museum, this site's main emphasis is on children's programming. Chesapeake Planetarium was the first planetarium to be built by a public school system and is open daily for school programs and one night each week for public shows.

Info in brief: A planetarium with an emphasis on children's programming.

Location: In the Chesapeake Municipal Center off I-64. (Near the site of the "Battle of Great Bridge" and a short distance from the Intracoastal Waterway.)

Hours: Contact planetarium for current schedule of programs.

Admissions: Public shows are free; group rate is $45. (It is recommended that children below the first grade level not be admitted to the planetarium chamber.)

Other sites of interest nearby: Virginia Beach beaches and hotels, American Revolution historic sites and more.

For further information write to Chesapeake Planetarium, P.O. Box 15204, Chesapeake, Virginia 23320, or call (804) 547-0143, Ext. 281.

The Children's Health Museum
Charlottesville, Virginia

The Children's Health Museum, established 11 years ago by the Junior League and the University of Virginia Medical Center, has as its main goal to serve children who are visiting the hospital for a variety of reasons. It is a small hands-on museum which encourages children ages 3 to 8 to learn about their bodies, health and the hospital experience in general.

One-on-one attention is the museum's main goal. After a child "checks in," a volunteer "adopts" him or her for the remainder of the visit and helps with the activities, which vary according to age. Activities include a ride in a child's wheelchair, a slide (dental health), a nutrition board, two anatomically correct dolls which help children learn about health and surgical procedures, hand and foot board, scales, "picket fence" (measure height), coordination board, X-ray box and distorted mirrors.

Many of the exhibits are portable and can be taken to classrooms for special workshops. School groups may also visit the museum itself, but small groups will be formed.

The museum is staffed by two full-time employees and more than 40 volunteers, including Junior League members, hospital personnel, and college students. The main goal for volunteers and staff alike is to help children learn that they do not have to be afraid of the hospital.

Info in brief: Hands-on, participatory exhibits with one-on-one attention a primary goal.

Location: Corner of the Primary Care Center of the University of Virginia's Health Sciences Center.

Hours: Monday–Friday, 9 A.M. to 4 P.M.

Admissions: Free.

For further information write to The Children's Health Museum, University of Virginia Health Sciences Center, Box 231-94, Charlottesville, Virginia 22908, or call (804) 924-1593.

Children's Museum of Virginia
Portsmouth, Virginia

The Children's Museum of Virginia displays interactive exhibits that encourage students to learn in a fun way about science, art, music, communication, technology and cultural diversity. The twelve main exhibit areas include "The City," "Science Circus," "Rock Climb," "Every Body," "Art Moves," "Blockbuster," "Bubbles," "Play Space," "New2Do Gallery," "You and Me," "Too Cool Gallery" and a Planetarium. Other special exhibits, activities, events and programs are also offered throughout the year.

Info in brief: Hands-on, interactive displays, grouped together by themes.

Location: In historic Olde Towne Portsmouth.

Hours: (Winter) Tuesday–Saturday, 10 A.M. to 5 P.M.; Sunday, 1 P.M. to 5 P.M. (Summer) Monday–Saturday, 10 A.M. to 7 P.M.; Sunday, 1 P.M. to 5 P.M. Closed most Mondays; open some holidays. Groups by reservation at other times.

Admissions: Small admissions charge. Memberships available. Under 14 must be accompanied by an adult.

Unique feature: The Children's Museum is within walking distance of four other museums that have banded together under the name of "Portsmouth Museums" (see below).

Other sites of interest nearby: Other Portsmouth museums — Naval Shipyard Museum (757) 393-8591, Lightship Museum (757) 393-8741, The Arts Center (757) 393-8543, and the Virginia Sports Hall of Fame (757) 393-8031. Many other Virginia tourist attractions are within a short driving distance.

For further information write to Children's Museum of Virginia, 221 High St., Portsmouth, Virginia 23704, or call (757) 393-8393 or 1-800-PORTS VA.

The Richmond Children's Museum
Richmond, Virginia

The Richmond Children's Museum opened its doors in 1981, offering a special place for children and their families in Central Virginia. Eleven main theme areas include Playworks, Children's Bank, Health & Safety Area, WRCM-TV Studio, SuperMarket!, Computer Station, The Cave, Art Studio, StagePlay, In My Own Backyard, and KidShop. All exhibits are hands-on and invite visitors to explore their world and its cultures from a child's perspective.

Special holiday activities, camp-ins, a Peanut Butter 'n Jam Family Concert Series and other special programs are also offered throughout the year. Visitors should contact the museum before visiting to get a current schedule of events.

Info in brief: A hands-on, exploratory museum for children and their caregivers.

Hours: (September–May) Monday, 9 A.M. to 5 P.M.; Tuesday–Friday, 9 A.M. to 1 P.M.; Saturday, 10 A.M. to 5 P.M.; Sunday, 1 P.M. to 5 P.M. (June–August) Monday–Friday, 9 A.M. to 5 P.M. Saturday and Sunday, same as winter hours.

Admissions: Call 1-800-KIDS-443 (543-7443) for current admissions charges.

Other sites of interest nearby: Science Museum of Virginia, Old Dominion Railway Museum, Busch Gardens–Williamsburg (in Williamsburg), Paramount's Kings Dominion (Doswell).

For further information write to The Richmond Children's Museum, 740 Navy Hill Dr., Richmond, Virginia 23219, or call (804) 644-3288 or FAX (804) 644-3281.

Science Museum of Western Virginia
Roanoke, Virginia

Established in 1970, the Science Museum of Western Virginia offers interactive exhibits for people of all ages. Included are two newly renovated galleries — The Science Arcade (with more than 40 interactive exhibits) and Body Tech: Science Behind Medicine. Other permanent exhibits include a weather station, Chesapeake Bay Touch Tank, Computers Then and Now and a simulated rainforest. At least one traveling exhibit is always on display. The Hopkins Planetarium, a 120-seat theater, is also part of the facility. Although it is not advertised as a children's museum *per se*, the type of exhibits and the atmosphere of the museum make it a true family-fun experience at which children will not be bored or frustrated.

Info in brief: A hands-on, interactive and participatory museum for people of all ages.

Location: Center in the Square building at 1 Market Square in Roanoke.

Hours: Monday–Saturday, 9 A.M. to 5 P.M.; Sunday, 1 P.M. to 5 P.M. Closed Thanksgiving, Christmas, and New Year's Day.

Admissions: Under 3, free; children (3–12), $3; seniors, $4; adults, $5. Planetarium is $1.30 extra with admission to museum; $2.60 for planetarium show only. Member ASTC.

Other sites of interest nearby: The Art Museum of Western Virginia (next door), Roanoke Valley History Museum (next door), Virginia's Transportation Museum, Mill Mountain Zoo, Virginia's Explore Park, Salem Museum, To the Rescue, and the Harrison Museum of African American Culture.

For further information write to the Science Museum of Western Virginia, One Market Square, Roanoke, Virginia 24011, or call (540) 342-5710 or FAX (540) 224-1240. Planetarium E-mail address: hopkins-planetarium@SMWV.org.

Shenandoah Valley Discovery Museum
Winchester, Virginia

For further information contact: Shenandoah Valley Discovery Museum, P.O. Box 239, 54 S. Loudoun St., Winchester, Virginia 22604, phone: (540) 722-2020. Member ASTC.

Virginia Discovery Museum
Charlottesville, Virginia

Opened in 1981, the Virginia Discovery Museum is located in the east end of the Downtown Mall (across from the post office).

Besides the regular exhibits, the museum offers various classes, special events and special activities throughout the year. An after-school science club for the whole family meets every Thursday with topics changing monthly.

In 1996 over 35,000 people visited the museum itself, with approximately 3,500 more people taking advantage of the special group tours and classes.

Permanent exhibits on display at the Virginia Discovery Museum include an 18th-century log house, "Virginia Faces" (a dress-up area), Playscape, an art studio, a computer lab, and a working beehive. Numerous rotating exhibits are changed around about every other month.

Info in brief: Hands-on science, history and art exhibits.

Location: East end of the Downtown Mall in Charlottesville, Virginia.

Hours: Tuesday–Saturday, 10 A.M. to 5 P.M.; Sunday, 1 P.M. to 5 P.M.; Closed Mondays; group reservations required.

Admissions: Ages 1–13, $3 (must be accompanied by an adult); adults, $4; seniors, $3; AAA discount, $.50. Memberships are offered. Member ASTC.

Unique exhibits or exhibitions: A complete 18th-century log house.

Other sites of interest nearby: Charlottesville tourist attractions.

For further information write to the Virginia Discovery Museum, P.O. Box 1128, Charlottesville, Virginia 22902, or call (804) 977-1025. Website: http://www.comet.net/vdm.

Virginia's Explore Park
Roanoke, Virginia

Virginia's newest museum is an authentic early 19th-century western Virginia settlement. Visitors see a working farm and a one-room country school in session. All visitors may pump the blacksmith's bellows, weave on a loom, help make furniture, help to harvest or plant a garden, cook in a fireplace, walk with the many farm animals from that time, and even help a Native American build an exact replica of an ancient lodge. Besides the hands-on activities, many craftsmen are at work for visitors to watch, and eight miles of trails can be hiked.

Info in brief: A village museum of interest to the whole family, but with more hands-on activities than most village museums offer.

Location: 1.5 miles off the Blue Ridge Parkway at mile post 115 (between U.S. 220 and St. Rte. 24); just 15 minutes from downtown Roanoke.

Hours: April–October, 9 A.M. to 5 P.M.

Admissions: Admissions charged. Contact the museum for current hours and admissions costs.

Unique exhibits: More hands-on activities for children than is usually offered in a village museum.

Other sites of interest nearby: The Chesapeake Bay Touch Tank, The Roanoke Valley History Museum, numerous festivals in the summer, Virginia's Transportation Museum, The Art Museum of Western Virginia, Mill Mountain Zoo, Salem Museum, To the Rescue, and the Harrison Museum of African American Culture.

For further information write to Virginia's Explore Park, P.O. Box 8508, Roanoke, Virginia 24014-8508, or call (540) 427-1800.

Washington

The Children's Activity Museum of Ellensburg
Ellensburg, Washington

Hours: Thursday–Saturday, 10 A.M. to 5 P.M.; Sunday, 1 P.M. to 5 P.M.

For further information write to The Children's Activity Museum of Ellensburg, 400 N. Main, Ellensburg, Washington 98926, or call (509) 925-6789.

The Children's Museum
Seattle, Washington

Opened in 1981 as a private nonprofit corporation, The Children's Museum (TCM) now has 23 full-time and 23 part-time employees who work with more than 130 volunteers to keep the museum running smoothly year-round. Through their efforts, the museum has won several national honors and awards.

The Children's Museum is located on the first level of Center House at Seattle Center. A recent expansion project stretched the museum space to 32,200 sq. ft., with 22,000 of that as exhibit space and 5,200 as program/activity space. TCM offers 12 permanent exhibit areas, two temporary exhibits, several year-round and seasonal programs and community outreach programming. Traditionally, the museum uses multicultural themes in the literary, visual and performing arts, including topics on illustrating, the environment, history and communication.

Info in brief: A hands-on museum (emphasizing the arts and humanities) which also offers numerous workshops and special programming throughout the year.

Location: Center House at Seattle Center, a municipally-owned park in Seattle.

Hours: Monday–Friday, 10 A.M. to 5 P.M.; Saturday and Sunday, 10 A.M. to 6 P.M. Summer hours are longer — contact the museum before visiting.

Admissions: Under 1, free; children, $5.50; adults, $4. Memberships are available.

For further information write to The Children's Museum, 305 Harrison St., Seattle, Washington 98109-4645, or call (206) 441-1768 or FAX (206) 448-0910.

Children's Museum of Snohomish County
Everett, Washington

The Children's Museum in Snohomish County provides interactive hands-on exhibits to children ages 2 to 12 and their families. The goal is to let them experience their community's history, culture, science and fine arts through these exhibits.

Activities included at the museum include experiencing an 1800s Snohomish County homestead, a hands-on creative art center, shopping in a French market and "cooking" in La Coupola, visiting the Magic School Bus and a new disabilities area, and more. Outreach programs are also offered.

Info in brief: Small hands-on museum especially for children.

Location: 3013 Colby, in Everett.

Hours: Tuesday–Saturday, 10 A.M. to 3 P.M. (Call about Monday attendance.)

Admissions: Under 2, free; all others, $2.

For further information write to Children's Museum in Snohomish County, P.O. Box 7621, Everett, Washington 98201, or call (206) 258-1006.

The Children's Museum of Tacoma
Tacoma, Washington

Hours: Tuesday–Friday, 10 A.M. to 5 P.M.; Saturday, 10 A.M. to 4 P.M.; Sunday, noon to 4 P.M. Open Monday, March–June.

For further information write to The Children's Museum of Tacoma, 925 Court C, Tacoma, Washington 98402, or call (206) 627-2436 or 627-6031.

Hands On Children's Museum
Olympia, Washington

The Hands On Children's Museum in Olympia is the only child-oriented resource center in Southwest Washington. It features interactive, hands-on exhibits in the arts and sciences for children 10 years of age and younger. Opening in 1993, the 2,300 sq. ft. museum has improved upon its exhibits every year. "The Fabulous Forest" is the newest major themed exhibit, teaching children and their families about the importance of the Northwest forests through demonstrations, hands-on experiments, machinery manipulation and creative activities.

Other exhibits include two computers with educational CD-ROM programs, creative theater activities, Soil Erosion table and corresponding experiments, and other activities available during special events.

Info in brief: A small hands-on museum with one major themed area and several smaller exhibits.

Location: 108 Franklin St., N.E. in Olympia.

Hours: Tuesday–Saturday, 10 A.M. to 5 P.M.

Admissions: Under 1, free; all others, $2.50.

Other sites of interest nearby: Olympia Farmers' Market (April–December), Wolf Haven International (wolf sanctuary with narrated tours), Percival Landing, Heritage Park Fountain, and the Washington State Capitol buildings and grounds.

Pioneer Farm Museum &
Ohop Indian Village
Eatonville, Washington

The Rainier Legacy supports The Pioneer Farm Museum, Ohop Indian Village and special outreach programs, using hands-on activities to "engage completely the five senses of 'children of any age' to experience our past and learn what we can become." Various tours are offered for large groups, but families and smaller groups have access to only one tour possibility at the Farm and one at the Village.

The Pioneer Farm Museum is a recreation of an 1880s settlement where children (and their caregivers) can tour log cabins, jump in the hay, pet animals and try other homesteader activities such as blacksmithing, woodworking, egg gathering, butter churning, wheat berry grinding, clothes scrubbing, and others.

The Ohop Indian Village offers visitors an opportunity to commune with nature in the woodlands, practicing hunting and fishing skills there, and then to return to the village to try preparing food items and working on winter craft activities, just as the Ohop Indians might have done.

Info in brief: A living history museum with an emphasis on hands-on learning.

Location: Between Hwy 161 and Hwy 7, 3 miles north of Eatonville in the Scenic Ohop Valley.

Hours: Summer (Fathers Day–Labor Day weekend) Pioneer Farm Tours — daily, 11 A.M. to 4 P.M. Native American Seasons Tour — Saturday and Sunday, 1 P.M. and 2:30 P.M. Trading Post — daily 10 A.M. to 5 P.M. Spring (March–Fathers Day week) and Fall (Labor Day–weekend before Thanksgiving) Pioneer Farm Tours — Saturday and Sunday, 11 A.M. to 4 P.M. Winter (Thanksgiving–February) Closed.

Admissions: (Priced per tour —$1 discount given when both tours are taken.) Children (3–18), $4.50; adults, $5.50; seniors (62+), $5.50.

Unique exhibitions: Large number of hands-on pioneering experiences available; all tours are guided only.

Other sites of interest nearby: The many tourist attractions in Seattle.

For further information write to The Rainier Legacy, 7716 Ohop Valley Road, Eatonville, Washington 98328, or call (360) 832-6300 or FAX (360) 832-4533.

Three Rivers Children's Museum
Kennewick, Washington

Hours: Tuesday–Saturday, 10 A.M. to 5 P.M.; Sunday, noon to 5 P.M.

For further information call the Three Rivers Children's Museum at (509) 783-6311.

Whatcom Children's Museum
Bellingham, Washington

The Whatcom Children's Museum is located in one of the four buildings which make up the Whatcom Museum of History and Art campus. The other three buildings offer exhibitions for all ages, including interactive components for children, but the one building is exclusively devoted to children and activities designed around their specific needs. The other buildings are the Syre Education Center, the Arco Exhibits Building and the main museum building. The main museum building is the Old City Hall, which is listed on the National Register of Historic Places.

The museums offer both permanent and changing exhibits throughout the year. They also offer education and enrichment programs. The staff includes 32 professional paid staff members along with over 800 active volunteers.

The Children's Museum opened in 1989 as the Children's Museum Northwest. It became a part of the Whatcom Museum of History and Art in 1992 and underwent a full-scale renovation in 1995. The Children's Museum now occupies a 4,500 sq. ft. building with more than 3,500 sq. ft. of exhibit space.

Info in brief: One of four separate museum buildings, this one is designated and designed specifically for young children, with hands-on exhibits emphasized.

Whatcom Children's Museum.

Location: Downtown cultural district of Bellingham on Prospect Street between Champion Street and Central Avenue.

Hours: Sunday, Tuesday and Wednesday, noon to 5 P.M.; Thursday, Friday and Saturday, 10 A.M. to 5 P.M. (Contact museum for hours of other buildings.)

Admissions: $2 per person for Children's Museum. Children must be accompanied by an adult. (Other buildings by donation.)

Unique exhibits: Four building set-up which can give a full day of museum visiting, both visual and tactile experiences being offered — visitors can look and do.

For further information write to the Whatcom Children's Museum, 227 Prospect St., Bellingham, Washington 98225, or call (360) 733-8769 or 676-6981.

World Kite Museum & Hall of Fame
Long Beach, Washington

The mission of the World Kite Museum & Hall of Fame, opened in 1990 in honor of the kite's 2,500-year-old history, is to tell the story of the kite by "preserving its past, recording its present, and honoring the people involved." The museum uses displays, education and activities to further this end. Various kite collections are displayed on a rotating schedule. Two new exhibits

are featured each year to highlight a single aspect of kite-related history or culture. Two permanent exhibits document the Washington State International Kite Festival and members of the Hall of Fame.

Although most of the exhibits themselves are not hands-on, the museum does plan to keep at least one changing exhibit running which will provide hands-on activities for children. All children visiting the museum are also allowed to wear traditional Japanese *hapi* coats while they go through the facilities. A variety of kite-making classes, hands-on flying demonstrations, elder hostel lectures and school field trips are also sponsored regularly. Plans are underway to increase the size of the current facility, at which time more interactive displays will be available.

Info in brief: A unique collections-type museum with at least one hands-on exhibit area for children. The content of the museum itself is also of special interest to children.

Location: Corner of 3rd St. North and Boulevard in Long Beach.

Hours: (June–August) daily, 11 A.M. to 5 P.M. (September–May) weekends, 11 A.M. to 5 P.M.

Admissions: Children, $.50; adults, $1; seniors, $.50; families, $3.

For further information write to The World Kite Museum and Hall of Fame, P.O. Box 964, Long Beach, Washington 98631 or call (360) 642-4020.

Yakima Valley Museum
Yakima, Washington

The mission of the Yakima Valley Museum is to promote an "understanding of Central Washington history as it affects the lives of contemporary citizens." Through the use of, for example, historic exhibits and art displays, the museum hopes to influence the future of Yakima Valley. These exhibits include "Historic Yakima," "Pioneer Life," "American Indian Culture and History," "Wagons, Carriages, and Coaches," "Natural History," special exhibitions, a research library, gift and book shop, and a new 1930s Art Deco Soda Fountain.

In 1996, the museum opened the new "Children's Underground." This 2,500 sq. ft. area is a special historical and educational hands-on area teaching children about the valley's past, present and future through the use of historic tools, household items, equipment, machines, and more. Available in this area are a freshwater trout aquarium, frog habitat, prehistoric exhibit, a "time tunnel" and opportunities to handle the historic objects and artifacts from the area.

Info in brief: A family-oriented museum with a large new children's hands-on area.

Location: Franklin Park.

Hours: (Museum) Monday–Friday, 10 A.M. to 5 P.M.; Saturday and Sunday, noon to 5 P.M.; (Children's Underground) Wednesday–Sunday, 1 P.M. to 5 P.M. (tours by appointment).

Admissions (includes museum and Children's Underground): 5 and under, free; students and seniors, $1.50; adults, $3; family, $7.

Unique exhibits: Special exhibitions and traveling exhibits change frequently.

Other sites of interest nearby: The historic H.M. Gilbert Homeplace; Union Gap Washington's historic attractions; Rail and Steam Museum (Toppenish); Yakima Indian National Cultural Center (Toppenish) and more.

For further information write to the Yakima Valley Museum, 2105 Tieton Dr., Yakima, Washington 98902, or call (509) 248-0747 or FAX (509) 453-4890. Website: http://www.wolfe.net/-museum or try museum@wolfenet.com.

Wisconsin

Discovery World Museum
The James Lovell Museum of
Science, Economics and Technology
Milwaukee, Wisconsin

Discovery World is the only science, economics and technology museum in Wisconsin and is named for James A. Lovell, commander of the Apollo 13 space mission who was raised in Milwaukee.

The idea for the museum was conceived in 1978 and has undergone numerous changes. The current 40,000 sq. ft. facility held its grand opening in October 1996 in the Museum Center, which also houses the Milwaukee Public Museum and the jointly-owned IMAX Dome Theater. The building consists of four stories with a copper foyer, classrooms and a small cabaret-style theater on the main level; exhibits on the second and third floors; a 160-seat theater on the third floor, and offices and workshops on the fourth floor. Exhibit areas include "Milwaukee Muscle: Simple Machines," "The Observatory," "Digital Thinkers," "Test Pilot Training," "Entrepreneur's Village," "Discovery World 4Cast Center," "Electricity & Magnetism," "Gears & Linkages," "Internal Combustion" and more.

More than 50 volunteers assist the 28 full-time and 20 part-time staff members to guide visitors through the hands-on and interactive displays. The staff also assist in outreach programs, Saturday workshops, special events and festivals and more.

Info in brief: An interactive, hands-on museum for children and their caregivers.

Location: In downtown Milwaukee in the new Museum Center. Discovery World shares its entrance with the Humphrey IMAX Dome Theater, and the Milwaukee Public Museum.

Hours: Daily, 9 A.M. to 5 P.M.

Admissions: Under 4, free; students (4–17), $3; adults (18–59), $5; seniors (60+), $4. Memberships available. Member ASTC.

Other sites of interest nearby: Milwaukee tourist attractions — Milwaukee has become the summer city of festivals. Contact the bureau of tourism there.

For further information write to Discovery World, 712 W. Wells St., Milwaukee, Wisconsin 53233, or call (414) 765-9966 or FAX (414) 765-0311. E-mail: hdq@braintools.org.

Great Explorations Children's Museum
Green Bay, Wisconsin

Great Explorations is a hands-on children's museum emphasizing the natural, technical and artistic aspects of their world. Exhibits include the "Mini Mart," "Wee Bank," "Wacky Wheels," "Investigation Station," "Healthy U," "The Locker Room," "The Play Park," "Tech-Know Junction," "Windows to the World," "Press-Gazette, Jr.," "From Pulp to Paper," "Imagination Station," "Oneida Past & Present," and "Water Works."

Info in brief: Hands-on, participatory museum exclusively for children and their caregivers.

Location: Port Plaza Mall in Green Bay.

Hours: Monday (by appointment only); Tuesday and Friday, 10 A.M. to 8 P.M.; Wednesday and Thursday, 10 A.M. to 5 P.M.; Saturday, 10 A.M. to 6 P.M.; Sunday, noon to 5 P.M.

Admissions: Under 2, free; others $3. No one under 17 admitted without an adult. Memberships available.

Other sites of interest nearby: Green Bay Packers attractions, Heritage Hill

State Historical Park, Hazelwood Historic Home Museum, New Zoo, Oneida Nation Museum, National Railroad Museum, Discovery Zone, and more.

For further information write to the Great Explorations Children's Museum, 320 North Adams Street, Green Bay, Wisconsin 54301, or call (414) 432-4397.

Madison Children's Museum
Madison, Wisconsin

The Madison Children's Museum is a private, nonprofit museum whose mission is to offer hands-on learning and fun for children and their families. The exhibits center around the themes of culture, science, technology and art.

Besides the permanent hands-on exhibits, the museum offers special events, activities and workshops throughout the year. Family fun is encouraged.

Originally opened in 1980 as a traveling museum, the new permanent museum site opened its doors in 1990. Now a two-story building, the museum offers more than seven permanent exhibits along with special exhibits on display during different times of the year. Permanent exhibits include "Leap into Lakes," "Lookagain Lane," "Shadow Room," "The Children of Chernobyl" (visual display), "Let's Grow," "Cows, Curds and Their Wheys," and "Brazil: Beyond the Rainforest."

Madison Children's Museum.

The museum also has developed the "Museum in a Shoebox Exchange Program" with Porto Alegre schoolchildren. This offers children in both countries the opportunity to be personally involved in different cultures.

Info in brief: Mostly hands-on exhibits, but various visual displays enhance the background and are meant to encourage critical thinking.

Location: Downtown Madison at the end of State Street, adjacent to the State Capitol building. Open only to city buses and bicycles, State Street contains unique shops, restaurants, coffee shops and the Children's Museum.

Hours: Tuesday–Sunday, 10 A.M. to 5 P.M.; Monday and holidays, closed. Open some Thursday evenings.

Admissions: Small admissions fee. Subsidy programs and special "free" hours are offered periodically.

Unique exhibits: Children of Chernobyl — displaying works of art created by children who live in the Chernobyl Zone. This exhibit is scheduled to close by 1998 to be replaced by more hands-on exhibits.

Other sites of interest nearby: State Street attractions, the State Capitol, five other museums within walking distance, and two lakes.

For further information write to Madison Children's Museum, 100 State Street, Madison, Wisconsin 53703 or call (608) 256-6445.

Milwaukee Public Museum
Milwaukee, Wisconsin

The Milwaukee Public Museum has welcomed visitors for more than 100 years and is one of Wisconsin's most popular attractions. In the museum's 150,000 sq. ft. of exhibit space, museum-goers can visit Africa, Asia, Europe, the Arctic, South and Middle America, the Pacific Islands and a Costa Rican rain forest. More than 6 million specimens and artifacts are on display, including life-size dinosaurs and their remains. Four floors of exhibits in the museum offer various interactive, educational programs. "Stop Spots," locations where educators are available to show artifacts and offer information relating to those exhibits, are placed regularly throughout the museum. A 6,500 sq. ft. exhibit, "A Tribute to Survival," serves as an introductory area for the museum's new North American Indian Wing. "Curiosity Zone" on the first floor offers the most hands-on interactive displays. An IMAX Dome Theater is also located at the facility.

Info in brief: A history museum (both cultural and natural), with numerous collections and one area designated as a hands-on, interactive area for children. One of the oldest and largest in the country. A new Humphrey IMAX Dome Theater is also on site.

Hours: Daily, 9 A.M. to 5 P.M. Closed Thanksgiving and Christmas Day and July 4th.

Admissions: Under 3, free; students (4–17 and with college ID), $3.50; adults, $5.50; seniors (60+), $4.50. Milwaukee County Residents with ID every Monday, free. Member ASTC.

Unique exhibit: World's largest known dinosaur skull and 6 million other specimens and artifacts.

For further information write to the Milwaukee Public Museum, 800 W. Wells St., Milwaukee, Wisconsin 53233 or call (414) 278-2700 or 2702 (TDD 278-2709). Website: http://www.mpm.edu. E-mail: Smedley@mpm1.mpm.edu.

Shawano County Historical Society Museum
Shawano, Wisconsin

The Shawano County Historical Society runs a museum which they describe as a "family" museum. They are listed as a children's museum, but their exhibits could not be evaluated.

For further information write to the Shawano County Historical Society, Inc., c/o Verona Owens, 417 E. 5th St., Shawano, Wisconsin 54166-2019.

Wyoming

Wyoming Territorial Prison
and Old West Park
Laramie, Wyoming

Formerly known as the Wyoming Territorial Park, the Wyoming Territorial Prison and Old West Park is a village museum which offers a variety of hands-on experiences especially for children. Most of these experiences occur in the Old West Frontier Town, and include panning for gold, joining a prison break posse, participating in a Pioneer Puppet Theatre, digging for dinosaur fossils, calf-roping, rope-making, taken a stagecoach ride, and visiting a petting corral.

Other "sights to see" in the town include the working blacksmith's shop, a medicine show, a fiddler, singers, livery stable, and more. The three other major areas of the park include guided tours of the Wyoming Territorial Prison, the National U.S. Marshals Museum, and a dinner theater. Many

Wyoming Territorial Prison and Old West Park.

special events are held in the park area during the year, so visitors should contact the park well in advance. Norma Slack, Calamity Jane's great, great niece, plays Calamity during numerous performances throughout the season.

Even though the prison is not a hands-on experience, it holds a great attraction for most children and their family members. It has been restored to its original 1890s condition, placed on the National Register of Historic Buildings, and is an important part of the rich Western history of the United States. The building has housed such prisoners as Butch Cassidy, Clark "The Kid" Pelton, Kich McKinney and Minnie Snyder. The National U.S. Marshals Museum is also historically significant.

Info in brief: Hands-on activities in the Wyoming Frontier Town only, but a full day of experiences are available throughout the entire park.

Location: Off I-80, 125 miles northwest of Denver, Colorado, and 120 miles northeast of Rocky Mountain National Park.

Hours: Dates, times and events are subject to change without notice. Call the park for exact information.

Admissions: General park entry is free; a small fee is charged to tour the Wyoming Territorial Prison and the National U.S. Marshals Museum. Reservations are required for the dinner theater.

Unique exhibits: Wyoming Territorial Prison.

For further information write to the Wyoming Territorial Prison and Old West Park, 975 Snowy Range Road, Laramie, Wyoming 82070, or call (307) 745-6161 or FAX (307) 745-8620. E-mail: wyoterprk@aol.com. Also look for their www page.

APPENDIX

Many museums are members of an association or associations which offer free admissions to visitors at other participatory museums which belong to the association. The most common association for children's museums is the AYM (Association of Youth Museums). Approximately 140 museums belong to this association, but not all of them offer special admissions privileges. For further information, write to:

> Association of Youth Museums
> 1775 K Street, NW
> Suite 595
> Washington, DC 20006

> or

> Call (202) 466-4144
> FAX (202) 466-4233
> E-mail aymdc@aol.com

In the Pacific Northwest, a group of museums have banded together to offer special admissions prices for museums in Oregon and Washington. All museums listed can provide visitors with a punch card which allows holders one free visit at every museum listed:

> The Children's Museum, Seattle, Washington
> The Children's Museum, Portland, Oregon
> The Children's Activity Museum of Ellensburg, Ellensburg, Washington
> The Gilbert House Children's Museum, Salem, Oregon
> Children's Underground/Yakima Valley Museum, Yakima, Washington
> Southern Oregon Historical Society Children's Museum, Jacksonville, Oregon
> Umpqua Discovery Center, Reedsport, Oregon
> Children's Museum of Snohomish County, Everett, Washington
> The Children's Carnegie Center, Oregon City, Oregon
> The Children's Museum of Tacoma, Tacoma, Washington
> Whatcom Children's Museum, Bellingham, Washington

Children's Museum of Eastern Oregon, Pendleton, Oregon
Hands On Children's Museum, Olympia, Washington
Oh! Zone Children's Museum, Joseph, Oregon
Three Rivers Children's Museum, Kennewick, Washington
Wonder Works, A Children's Museum, Two Dalles, Oregon
Willamette Science & Technology Center (WISTEC), Eugene, Oregon

Another large association is the Association of Science-Technology Centers Incorporated (ASTC). This is an international association and includes more than just children's museums. The Reciprocal Free Admission Program (RFAP) entitles visitors to free general admission to any ASTC museum, but does not include admissions to planetariums, large-screen theater presentations or any special programs offered by an individual museum. To obtain a list of participating museums, you must contact an ASTC museum. Membership in one participating museum provides membership in the RFAP.

There are many other associations available, including VAM (Virginia Association of Museums) and AAM (American Association of Museums). It is strongly suggested that you contact your local or nearby museum to find out about membership there, and ask about reciprocal programs with other museums.

As stated in this book's Introduction, many small museums have a very tight budget and choose not to pay any association fees. This does not mean, however, that families cannot have a great visit. Caregivers are encouraged to teach their children that there are things to be learned from any and all experiences, and that they do not have to go to EPCOT or Disney World to have a great time.

INDEX